Giannis Antetokounmpo: The Inspiring Story of One of Basketball's Rising Superstars

An Unauthorized Biography

By: Clayton Geoffreys

Visit my website at www.claytongeoffreys.com
Cover photo by Keith Allison is licensed under CC BY 2.0 / modified from original

Table of Contents

Foreword

As of today, we have entered one of the best time periods to be alive and watching basketball. The sport has reached an all-time high in popularity, and the talent in the league is rivaled by only a few other historical time periods of the sport. Many young stars are rising in the league, but few capture as much attention as Giannis Antetokounmpo. Since joining the league as a relatively unknown international player, Giannis has quickly developed into one of the most promising future superstars due to his ability to cause a variety of defensive matchup nightmares and sheer athleticism. It will be exciting to see what the Bucks are able to accomplish in the coming years as their young core begins maturing into the prime of their careers. Thank you for purchasing *Giannis Antetokounmpo: The Inspiring Story of One of Basketball's Rising Superstars*. In this unauthorized biography, we will learn Giannis Antetokounmpo's incredible life story and impact on the game of basketball. Hope you enjoy and if you do, please do not forget to leave a review!

Also, check out my website at claytongeoffreys.com to join my exclusive list where I let you know about my latest books. To thank you for your purchase, you can go to my site to download a free copy of *33 Life Lessons: Success Principles, Career Advice & Habits of Successful People*. In the book, you'll learn from some of the greatest thought leaders of different industries on what it takes to become successful and how to live a great life.

Cheers,

Clayton Geoffreys

Visit me at www.claytongeoffreys.com

Introduction

The NBA loves rags to riches stories about how a person that lived and grew up in poverty worked to get to the league, not only as an ordinary player, but as a superstar ranking among the best in the world. These are the stories that make people adore the player and what he has been through to get to the top. More importantly, these are the stories that inspire young children to work just as hard, if not harder, than their idol to reach the success that they aspire to achieve.

Several of the greatest players in league history have had to endure poverty before they found success in the NBA. Allen Iverson barely had a home growing up before he starred at Georgetown. In his MVP speech back in 2014, Kevin Durant said that his mother raised him and his brother alone while the family moved from roof to roof. The same was true for LeBron James, who was raised alone by his mother when she was only 16 years old. These players not only earned millions as NBA superstars but have also become fan favorites because of how they worked their way up to get to the league.

Likewise, the NBA has also found a liking for players that were seemingly genetically engineered to dominate in basketball. These are the players that, at a glance, were naturally destined to be great because of the physical tools they possess. If the NBA was a horse race, these players are your thoroughbreds judging by how much more physically gifted and talented they are than the rest of the competition.

A lot of the world's greatest players have been gifted with natural physical talents that have helped them forge Hall of Fame careers. You can mention guys like Wilt Chamberlain and Shaquille O'Neal, who were both bigger and more athletic than their counterparts in the league. Standing at least seven feet tall, Dirk Nowitzki has the skills and shooting stroke of a guard. Yao Ming was a 7'6" giant that could move faster than his size would let on. And at 6'9", Magic Johnson moved like and had the skills of a player nine inches shorter than he is. These are the players that have been called "freaks of nature," not because of their appearances, but because of their freakish physical gifts that make them nearly unguardable in the league. Likewise, these players have also become favorites because of the seemingly unnatural things they do on the floor.

In today's NBA, one player has had to undergo poverty and a life of hardship while also possessing physical tools that made it seemed like he was destined for greatness. He grew up a poor boy far away from the NBA, but his height and basketball potential were what saved him from living in poverty. That player is Giannis Antetokounmpo.

Giannis Antetokounmpo was not your typical poor kid that was obsessed with basketball at a young age who tried to develop from there. He was the son of Nigerian immigrants that struggled to find a job in Greece. Because of that, basketball was not even on his radar. Giannis had to do what he could to try to support his family as a young boy. He had to live one of the most poverty-stricken childhoods among all of today's NBA players.

But it was evident that Giannis Antetokounmpo was going to move past his life of poverty because of the physical gifts he had. At age 18, he tried his hand at the NBA Draft. His measurements astonished scouts. At such a young age, Antetokounmpo was already as tall as 6'9" and had a wingspan of at least 7'3". The scary part was that he was still growing. Because of his height and length, it took no time for him to be dubbed as "The Greek Freak."

However, Giannis Antetokounmpo was not an instant star like Shaq, Magic, LeBron, and KD were the moment they got to the league. Giannis was, in fact, an unknown because the only exposure he had to the basketball world was in Greece. Few people in the United States were familiar with him and his skills. He was even only drafted 15th in the 2013 NBA Draft. People could not even pronounce his name to the point that he was also nicknamed "The Alphabet" since his name seemingly had all 24 letters of the alphabet. But the team that drafted him, the Milwaukee Bucks, knew they had a gem in Antetokounmpo.

A lot of NBA players are even taller and longer than Giannis Antetokounmpo. However, what they did not have was the mobility and skills of the Greek Freak. Antetokounmpo moved quickly for a player of his height. At the small forward position, he could even handle the ball as well as most guards in the league. It was like the Bucks were already thinking that they had the second coming of Magic Johnson. Giannis had all of the physical tools to be great. The problem was that he was coming into the league as a very raw prospect.

Since coming into the NBA, Giannis Antetokounmpo made significant improvements that were as long as the strides he could make on the court. Remarkably, he was still growing. Giannis peaked at a height of 6'11", which is two inches more than his draft measurements in 2013. It was also clear how much he worked on his body. Coming in as skinny as a twig, Antetokounmpo packed on serious muscle mass over the years to become a solid physical specimen.

While he made significant improvements on his body since getting drafted, Giannis improved even more on his skills. Originally slated as a player that had good physical tools to defend all five positions on the floor, Antetokounmpo grew leaps and bounds on his offense. He improved his ball-handling skills as well as his offense to become a reliable scorer at the small forward position. And after getting trained as a point guard as early as his third season in the NBA, Giannis Antetokounmpo showed flashes of what he can do as an all-around player by registering numerous triple-doubles, which is a rarity for someone standing 6'11".

By the time Antetokounmpo reached his fourth season in the NBA, he had already blossomed into a star by making his first All-Star appearance. His numbers spoke for themselves. As the superstar of the Milwaukee Bucks, he averaged more than 20 points, nearly nine rebounds, and over five assists to show how much he had improved since his rookie season when he was still one of the rawest prospects in the league.

However, that was not yet Giannis' peak as he suddenly grew from a skinny and raw prospect during his rookie year to the most dominant player in the league. He became the ultimate double-double machine and a player that could affect both ends of the floor at a stellar level because of his unique combination of size, length, strength, athleticism, mobility, and skills.

By the time he reached his sixth season in the league, Giannis Antetokounmpo was dominant. He was easily dunking over the opposition and was simply unstoppable when he got to the painted area. And from a raw prospect that struggled to make ends meet, he became the NBA's top MVP contender and the flagship superstar for the league's future.

Still in his mid-20s, Giannis Antetokounmpo has already reached heights that only his long arms can reach. He is the NBA's most unstoppable player and is only going to get better in the coming years. His potential is through the roof and is even higher than people originally thought. And if he does reach the height of his powers, the NBA better watch out.

Chapter 1: Childhood and Early Life

Giannis Antetokounmpo was born in Athens, Greece on December 6, 1994, to Charles and Veronica Antetokounmpo, who migrated from Nigeria all the way to Greece. Charles was a former soccer player while Veronica was a high-jumper. However, both Charles and Veronica were illegal immigrants to Greece. As such, Giannis and two of his other brothers, who were also born in Greece, had no citizenship and were neither Nigerian nor Greek.

Living in Greece, Charles and Veronica struggled to find jobs because of the illegality of their stay in the country and because their only work background was their life as athletes back in Nigeria. Because of that, Giannis and his older brother Thanasis had to help their parents make a living. The Antetokounmpo brothers spent their days on the streets peddling sunglasses, watches, toys, and souvenir tickets, hungry and desperate for money to help the family pay the bills and buy groceries.[i]

Money was not the only problem that the Antetokounmpo family faced during those hard times. Both Charles and Veronica lived in fear that the police might one day find them, ask them for their papers, and deport them back to Nigeria. And because of their failure to promptly pay rent, the family would often bounce from home to home.

For Giannis Antetokounmpo, such a hard childhood living in Greece in poverty is something he keeps to heart because it was how he learned to work as hard as he does now. "I can't push it to the side. I can't say, 'I've made it, I'm done with all that.' I will always carry it with me. It's where I learned to work like this," were his exact words. He would spend all day selling items and singing carols for tourists during Christmas but would come home empty-handed on some days. Giannis said that it was never guaranteed that he could make money off of what he did, but it was his best chance.[ii] It was this same attitude of resilience and hard work that kept him coming back to the gym to improve when he became an NBA player.

Even when Giannis Antetokounmpo was a young boy, everybody else could already see his pedigree as a future pro athlete. His customers would often comment about his freakishly long limbs, but Giannis could not care any less about his physical abilities, athleticism, or potential. All he cared about was someone buying the items he was selling. All he cared about was working hard as the Greek Peddler rather than becoming the Greek Freak.[ii] He never cared what his body was telling him other than that it needed food. He never understood what it meant being as physically gifted as he was because he was thinking about finding a penny for his next meal.

But fate would come into play one day in 2008. Thanasis was spending an afternoon in a field in the neighborhood of Sepolia kicking a soccer ball around. He would pique the interest of a basketball coach who just happened to be in the neighborhood at the time. However, the coach did not bother to talk to the older Antetokounmpo until one day his club was in search of fresh new talent.[iii]

The coach returned to the neighborhood to ask about the tall boy he saw. He found his name but would nevertheless fail to find him. Instead, what he found was better. The basketball coach named Spiros Velliniatis spotted the then 13-year-old Giannis with his brothers Kostas and Alexis on that same field playing soccer. He was immediately charmed by the physical capabilities of the skinny boys, who seemed taller and longer than most other teenagers their age. The first thing he asked himself was how anyone could have overlooked Giannis' physical skill. He would go on to think that Giannis was going to be one of the best basketball talents in the world.[iii] He immediately invited the boys to play basketball despite how reluctant they were to join practices.

Velliniatis was a coach of the basketball club Filathlitikos, which was located in a neighborhood far from Sepolia, where the Antetokounmpos lived. It was difficult for the coach to entice the two young brothers to join practices because of their lack of interest in the sport and because they would rather spend time earning money to help the household. But Velliniatis gave them an offer that was hard to refuse. He told Giannis that he would join the club if he could find jobs for his parents. The young Antetokounmpo responded positively.[iii]

Giannis and Thanasis would try out for Filathlitikos, but what stood out was the younger Antetokounmpo's drive and hunger to work harder for success. This was what convinced team management to try to keep Giannis on their team despite many factors that would otherwise prevent him from doing so. At that time, basketball was the least of Giannis Antetokounmpo's interests. He found soccer the more entertaining sport.[iv] After all, his father played professional soccer back in Nigeria. But when it came to basketball, Giannis hardly knew anything about the game or its rich history. On the other hand, Thanasis wanted to become a track and field star.

Other than that, the family was also battling through poverty. Filathlitikos was practicing in another neighborhood, which made it more costly for the family to have them join practices far away. They also did not have enough money to keep the boys nourished before and after practices. But neighbors tried to help with what they could. Notably, Giannis Tsikas, a local cafe owner, prepared meals for the two boys to prevent them from starving before practices.[iv]

To help battle the family's poverty, Velliniatis found a way to give the family some support. Filathlitikos' management and board members chipped in to provide

500 euros monthly to the family so that they could have Giannis and his brother with the team. According to Velliniatis, that was the first time they had to sponsor a 13-year-old to join the team.[iii] But it was not an ordinary 13-year-old. That kid was Giannis Antetokounmpo, a soon-to-be NBA All-Star.

At first, Giannis Antetokounmpo was all potential with no skill. He could not even make a layup with his height and length. But while other kids and teenagers had the necessary skills and fundamentals all mastered, they did not have what Giannis had. Antetokounmpo came in with physical potential. He had the height and length to one day dominate basketball. On top of all that, he practiced and worked hard like he had a chip on his shoulder. For him, the practices seemed like a job that he needed to keep to feed his family.

Family was what kept Giannis Antetokounmpo practicing for the children, teen, and adult teams of Filathlitikos. He wanted to keep his family fed with the sustenance that they were receiving from Filathlitikos. He could not quit for that reason alone, though there were several times he wanted to stop. Giannis wanted to be a soccer player and not a basketball star. He only stayed with Filathlitikos for his family. After a year of practicing, he even decided to stop attending practices because he was uninterested in the game at that time in his life.[iii]

One day, Velliniatis convinced Giannis to stay with the team by telling him to give it his best, and if he ultimately still failed, he would take him to a soccer team. At that time, people thought that Velliniatis was crazy for fighting tooth and nail just to keep an uninterested kid in the team. But all of that changed when the 15-year-old Giannis Antetokounmpo scored 50 points in his first ever official basketball game. That was when Giannis and everyone else knew that he was bound for stardom.[iii]

Even back then, Velliniatis already saw the makings of a star in Giannis Antetokounmpo, not because of his physical talents, but because of how desperately hard he worked. As the coach would say, Giannis was not a child back then. He never acted like one because he was forced to survive and mature ever since the day he was born. It made him tough, competitive, and fierce. Every game, it was as if Antetokounmpo had something to prove. It was as if he wanted to destroy his opponents.[iii] It was what a hard childhood life taught him to do. This life lesson made Giannis Antetokounmpo a hardworking future NBA star.

News of how Giannis Antetokounmpo was dominating the competition back in Greece circulated the world. It made as far as the Boston Celtics' Danny Ainge's ears. Giannis was not playing in Greece's top league. However, that did not stop people from wondering what the then 18-year-old phenom could do. After all, Dirk Nowitzki, who did not play in Germany's top division, walked down the same path but ended up becoming an all-time great.

Considering how less distant other European countries were, the eyes that would pay the closest attention to Giannis Antetokounmpo were not from the NBA, but from other top leagues near the region. The first team to make an offer to the rising teenager was Zaragoza, a basketball club based in Spain. Zaragoza offered Giannis 400,000 euros a year, which was a lot more than the 500 euros a month that his parents were making in Greece.

Giannis Antetokounmpo was excited about the thought of going to Spain. He wanted to take his family there and live a life better than they did in Greece. He immediately signed the contract, which would have made him a professional player in Spain. However, the contract had a clause that would ultimately give him a much better career than he would have had in Spain. It had a buyout clause that allowed him to escape the contract if he was drafted into the NBA. Luckily for Giannis, he made it to the big leagues.

Chapter 2: NBA Career

Getting Drafted

Due to the experience and following he had earned in Greece, Giannis Antetokounmpo got the attention of NBA scouts that were marveled by what potential he may hold. Because of that, Antetokounmpo was not content with playing professional basketball in Greece or any part of Europe. He wanted to try his hand in the NBA where the biggest basketball dreams happen.

Every scout and general manager that had the opportunity to watch and see Giannis Antetokounmpo were all initially in awe of his physical talents. That was the thing that stood out about Antetokounmpo at glance even without knowing how much he worked on his craft. At 18 years old, Giannis stood 6'9" and had a wingspan of 7'3". His hands were among the biggest ever measured in the NBA. Giannis Antetokounmpo's hands measured 12 inches. They were bigger than Kawhi Leonard's, who is famous for his massive mitts.[v]

While there have been a lot of NBA players with the same or even better physical attributes than Giannis Antetokounmpo had, what set the Greek teenager apart was his mobility and athleticism. With his length and strides, he seemed to be gliding out on the floor and could reach the other end in a heartbeat. He moved a lot better than players of his size, much like how Kevin Durant does at 6'10". On top of that, he also had mad hops that reportedly took him as high as 40" off the ground. Because of his mobility and athleticism, Giannis Antetokounmpo looked fluid out on the floor and it seemed that he was just as tall as smaller guards.

The most glaring part of Giannis Antetokounmpo's physical attributes was not how tall he was during his draft measurements, but how much taller and longer he could still be when it was all said and done. At 18 years old, he was already tall at 6'9". At that young age, he had not reached his peak height. Even doctors said that he still had enough growth years left in him to reach 7 feet.[vi] With that fluid athleticism and length combined, Giannis Antetokounmpo was a scary prospect as far as physical talents were concerned.

Offensively, Giannis Antetokounmpo benefited a lot from his size and length when he was in Greece scoring against smaller and shorter defenders. With his long strides, he could get to the basket in only a few steps before the defenders could react. He could finish strong at the basket because of his mobility, athleticism, body control, and length.

On the break, Giannis Antetokounmpo was unstoppable in Greece. He moved so quickly and so fluidly that he could get from end to end in the heartbeat. It was even shown that he could do so with only two or three dribbles because of how long his strides are. And when he gets to the other end, he has enough momentum and length in him to finish strong in the paint.[vii]

Antetokounmpo's best offensive skill is not his ability to score and finish, but his talents as a playmaker. Using his freakishly huge hands, Giannis can control the ball well with one hand. He has good enough handles to take the ball down the court and drive to the basket. He handles the ball well despite his size and length.

On top of Giannis Antetokounmpo's handles, he had also shown good enough passing abilities that could make him a point forward in the NBA when he got to that level. His basketball IQ seems high enough to make him a playmaker while his instincts at making the right pass belie his inexperience as a teenage basketball player. He shows creativity at reading defenses and making the right plays and passes well enough for a man of his age.[v]

The defensive end was where most scouts believed he could excel the most in the NBA. With that much height, length, mobility, and athleticism, Giannis Antetokounmpo is one of the rare players that can guard four positions out on the floor. He can keep up laterally with guards while also making it hard for them to get around his length. He can go toe-to-toe with wingmen because of his length and size. And in the paint, he can intimidate and even get blocked shots because of his length and leaping ability.

Giannis has also shown great instincts as a defender. He knows how to use his superior length in getting his hands in the passing lanes. He knows how to read passes and make the steal when it was time for him to do so, much like how he knows how to read defenses whenever he makes plays. Giannis Antetokounmpo has also shown good instinct in making blindside blocks with great timing and accuracy.[vii]

With so much athleticism, length, and mobility at his size, Giannis Antetokounmpo was often regarded as the next coming of someone like Nicolas Batum, who is similar in length and body build but can also make plays and bring the ball down. Batum has also shown the ability to become an elite defender in the league. However, the difference was that Giannis Antetokounmpo is most effective whenever he has the ball in his hands. On the other hand, Batum can do just as much damage off the ball as when he does handling.

The one main reason why Giannis Antetokounmpo was never great off the ball was his poor shooting accuracy. On the offensive end, he was still so raw and inexperienced that he had only refined a few skills. He does have the potential to become a good shooter, but his mechanics are still off. With his length and athleticism, he would have been a threat from the perimeter, much like how unguardable Kevin Durant is when pulling up. However, Giannis' jump shot still seemed to be a work in progress coming into the draft.

Giannis Antetokounmpo had not showcased the ability to create his shots. Most of Giannis' scoring came from the transition or when he could blow past his man with his long strides. However, he had not yet refined his shot-making skills, though he had enough ball handling talents to help him in that category. Even when he had his feet planted on the ground, he still struggled to get shots from the perimeter.[v]

On the defensive end, Giannis had the potential to become one of the best. However, he still lacked basic defensive fundamentals because of his inexperience. Giannis tended to be too upright instead of keeping a low base whenever he defended the perimeter. His defensive stance needed a lot of work.[v] Giannis had also shown that he lacked proper positioning on the defensive end while also failing to comprehend his assignments' movements out on the floor. This allowed more experienced players to beat him out whenever they had him guarding them.

Physically, Giannis Antetokounmpo needed to work a lot on his body. He was coming into the draft at a skinny 195 pounds. Even players a lot shorter than he was were stronger and heavier. After growing up in poverty and training without the facilities and equipment that most other clubs had, Antetokounmpo had no opportunity to bulk up his body. With such a skinny frame, he would find it difficult to finish strong against bigger defenders in the NBA. He might even struggle defensively when guarding against more physical and strong opponents such as a LeBron James. Even on off the ball plays like setting screens, Giannis might struggle because of his lack of heft, strength, and width.[v]

The biggest challenge for Giannis Antetokounmpo when trying to pack on some weight in the NBA was maintaining the same level of mobility, fluidity, and athleticism. A lot of players have struggled to stay mobile when adding size. Boris Diaw was quick and mobile during his younger and skinnier days but has since struggled to be as athletic as he was when he added heft to his body. Antetokounmpo might one day face the same trouble if he failed to make his body adjust to the added weight.

Giannis Antetokounmpo's most glaring weakness is his inexperience. A lot of NBA prospects learned the game at a young age. At age 13, Antetokounmpo did not know how to play basketball. He did not even know some of the biggest names in NBA history. He learned the game at a late age and did not have the chance to develop his experience. On top of that, Giannis Antetokounmpo was playing in the A2 division, which was not even Greece's toughest league. He did not face the best players that Greek basketball had to offer while settling for competition with the country's younger and less talented players.

Because of his inexperience, Giannis remained raw and unpolished. He often showed a lot of mental lapses and mistakes while also making questionable decisions that more experienced players would not have made. His mentality and upbringing as a playmaker also led to a lack of a killer instinct to the point that he would always want to get his teammates involved even in situations where he was supposed to take over.[v]

While it may not necessarily be a weakness, another problem with Giannis Antetokounmpo was that he had yet to establish himself at one or two playing positions. In Greece, his development came before creating a proper playing position. He started as a power forward but acted like a small forward out on the perimeter whenever he did not have the ball. And when he had the ball, he was out on the top of the key like a point guard should be despite the fact that he was the tallest player. It may not be a weakness to be a jack of all trades per se, but Antetokounmpo might not have developed a proper go-to skillset in the NBA if the focus was on him playing all five positions on the floor.

With all of that on the table, Giannis Antetokounmpo was an intriguing prospect in a 2013 NBA Draft that did not seem like the most talented batch of soon-to-be NBA rookies. The Cleveland Cavaliers had the top overall pick but chose to pluck Anthony Bennett out of UNLV. Bennett was a huge bust and did not make a role player's impact on the league. Other notable lottery picks included Victor Oladipo (second), Otto Porter (third), and Michael Carter-Williams (11th), who was named Rookie of the Year after peaking in his first year in the league. However, none of the top fourteen players were even close to becoming All-Stars in the league. The draft class lacked talent and potential. Then there was Giannis Antetokounmpo.

Antetokounmpo was an unknown though scouts had heard his name and seen him play. The problem was that he was not tested enough against tough competition. Players drafted before him were not as physically gifted as he was, nor did they have his potential. However, they were tested in competition far tougher than Giannis had in Greece. For most teams, Antetokounmpo looked like a long-term raw project that could not immediately pay dividends. But the Milwaukee Bucks took him with the 15th pick anyway.

The story of how Giannis fell into the hands of the Milwaukee Bucks is an interesting one. A few months before the draft, Bucks general manager John Hammond was in a tough situation. The Bucks were a fighting team that worked hard, but they did not have a star. Attempts at making a star in Milwaukee were all unsuccessful. From Andrew Bogut to Brandon Jennings and Monta Ellis, there were no players that blossomed into stars in Milwaukee. The last All-Star they had was Michael Redd in 2006. Some may even think that Redd just had a fluke of a season back then.

John Hammond knew the chances of landing a star through a high lottery pick was slim because they had low chances of getting the top overall pick. And nobody wanted to play for the small and frigid market of Milwaukee, either. If Hammond wanted to get a star to the Bucks, he had to look in a place nobody else would. He had to go to Greece.

Hammond was not the only one interested in scouting Giannis Antetokounmpo, however. The Atlanta Hawks had connections with the young teen's agent. They offered the agent a job with the organization if Antetokounmpo did not get drafted ahead of their 17th pick. Other teams also wanted to draft him in the second round and stash him in Europe much like how the Spurs did with Manu Ginobili more than a decade back.[i]

But Hammond had the advantage of having the 15th pick in the draft. He spent three days personally looking at the beanstalk kid from Athens before he finally decided that he was going to change Giannis Antetokounmpo's life. He was going to draft him and make him the biggest steal of the 2013 NBA Draft to the surprise of everyone in the league. The rest became history as Giannis eventually landed with Milwaukee.

After being drafted by an NBA team, Giannis Antetokounmpo never got to play for Zaragoza in Spain because the Bucks chose to exercise the buyout clause in the contract he had signed. In just his rookie season in the NBA, he would be making nearly four times as much as he would have in Zaragoza. He could afford his family what they needed, had finally gotten himself out of poverty, and was living the American dream.

Rookie Season

Getting drafted by the Milwaukee Bucks was not an easy situation for Giannis Antetokounmpo to be in. The Bucks were in a rebuilding phase and identity crisis regarding the decision on who to keep for the future and who to put their hopes on. At that time, they were relying more on point guard Brandon Knight and a core group of long players that included Khris

Middleton, John Henson, and Ersan Ilyasova. Based on player profile and length, Giannis Antetokounmpo fit right in.

Giannis Antetokounmpo made his NBA debut on October 30, 2013, at barely 19 years old. In that loss to the New York Knicks, he played less than five minutes and scored a single point off a free throw. The following game, which was versus the Boston Celtics, he got his first taste of NBA victory in a win. He had five points and two rebounds in 12 minutes of action that game. A day later, he saw his minutes increased to 17 when the Bucks suffered a loss against the Toronto Raptors. He had two points, two rebounds, and one steal in that outing.

In the next two games for the Milwaukee Bucks, the long and tall rookie would not make appearances due to the coach's decision. The first game was a win over the Cleveland Cavaliers on November 6 followed by a loss to the Dallas Mavericks three days later.

Giannis saw a return to the court on November 12 to play the fourth game of his NBA career. In that loss to the Miami Heat, he earned valuable experience playing against the defending champions and LeBron James, who was considered the best player in the world at that time. Antetokounmpo had his then-best game as a professional player in the NBA by racking up 11 points and four rebounds. Often regarded as a raw player that needed a lot of work on his jumper, Antetokounmpo hit three of his five three-pointers in that game.

After that game against the Heat, Antetokounmpo found himself playing consistent bench minutes for the Milwaukee Bucks, who just kept losing game after game. He then missed two more games on November 20 and 22 before seeing 12 minutes of action and scoring six points in each game of the Bucks' bouts against the Charlotte Bobcats and Detroit Pistons. The Bucks' losing streak would extend to 11 against Charlotte on November 29. Antetokounmpo had four points in only 13 minutes of play that game. In snapping the losing streak against the Boston Celtics on November 30, Giannis had the second double-digit scoring game of his career after going for ten points on 4 out of 6 shooting from the floor. He also added then-career highs of seven rebounds and four assists in nearly 28 minutes of play.

That win over the Boston Celtics started the turning point of what was otherwise a bleak and uneventful rookie season for Giannis Antetokounmpo. He suddenly started seeing increases in his minutes and usage on the floor on the offensive end. But Giannis Antetokounmpo did not just see a clear increase in playing time.

By that time of the season, Giannis Antetokounmpo, who just turned 19 years old, made an announcement that he had grown to stand a little over 6'10". Several months back when he was getting measured for the NBA Draft, he was an 18-year-old 6'9" forward. In less than a season, he had grown an inch and a quarter while also revealing that team doctors projected him to grow as much as two more inches to become a legitimate 7-footer.[vi]

The now taller and longer Giannis Antetokounmpo put his height and length to good use in a career performance against the San Antonio Spurs on December 11. Playing a new career best of 33 minutes in that game, he put up career numbers of 15 points, eight rebounds, and two steals. Giannis made five of his eight field goal attempts in that game.

Two days later, Antetokounmpo performed well again after going for eight points and a new career best of nine rebounds in a one-point loss to the Chicago Bulls. After that, he scored in double digits for the fourth time that season after going for 13 points on 3 out of 9 shooting from the floor in a loss to the Dallas Mavericks. Giannis played 35 minutes that game.

In a double-overtime classic against the New York Knicks on December 18, Giannis Antetokounmpo's toughness and stamina were put to the test. Starting for the first time in his career, Antetokounmpo was matched up against superstar scoring forward Carmelo Anthony, who was shorter but more physically imposing. Using his length against Carmelo, who favored shooting perimeter jumpers, Giannis limited his matchup to a dismal 9 out of 29 shooting from the field. Though he fouled out and the Bucks ended up losing that game, Giannis finished with ten points and seven rebounds in nearly 42 minutes of play. His defensive work against Anthony was what kept the Bucks alive in that game.

After that performance, Giannis Antetokounmpo started to see consistent minutes as a starter while also getting more involved on the offensive end for the Bucks. In a win over the Philadelphia 76ers on December 21, he had 12 points and seven rebounds while shooting 3 out of 7 from the field. Two nights later, he had 12 points again in a loss to the Bobcats

On December 27, Giannis Antetokounmpo truly broke out. In what was then his best performance all season long, the "Greek Freak" put up his first double-double game of 16 points and ten rebounds in a loss to the Brooklyn Nets. Since then, his confidence on both ends of the floor only grew more as the season progressed. He even had four steals and two blocks the following night in a loss to the Minnesota Timberwolves.

In the final game of an eventful and life-changing 2013 for Giannis Antetokounmpo, the Greek Freak grabbed a career high of 11 rebounds when the Milwaukee Bucks defeated the Los Angeles Lakers on December 31. Giannis also added eight points on 3 out of 7 shooting in that game.

On January 11, Giannis Antetokounmpo got his first double-double of the New Year. He had 13 points, 11 rebounds, five assists, two steals, and two blocks for what was an all-around game for him in that loss to the Oklahoma City Thunder. That was also the first time he had to match up with Kevin Durant, who he was often compared to from a physical standpoint, for an entire game. Durant, however, got the best of Giannis in that matchup. After that loss to the Thunder, Giannis would score in double digits three more times until the Bucks won their first game of 2014. In that win over the Detroit Pistons, he had four points and five rebounds in only 25 minutes of play.

However, Giannis would later lose his starting spot after coach Larry Drew decided to go with a smaller lineup with little-known Nate Wolters at the second guard position and Khris Middleton taking Antetokounmpo's small forward spot. Nevertheless, Giannis remained an integral part of the rotation. The Bucks' next win would be seven games later on February 3. In that match, Giannis Antetokounmpo finished with 15 points on 5 out of 9 shooting against the New York Knicks.

During All-Star Weekend, Giannis Antetokounmpo felt what it is like playing with some of the best players the world has to offer as he made his way New Orleans to take part in the 2014 Rising Stars Challenge. As a member of Team Grant Hill, Giannis played 17 minutes and made all three of his field goal attempts to score nine points in a win over Team Chris Webber. And despite his size, he was a participant in the Skills Challenge.

Giannis Antetokounmpo would then score in double digits twice in February after the All-Star break. He had 11 points in a loss to the Denver Nuggets on the 20th before registering 13 points, six rebounds, and four assists in a win over the Philadelphia 76ers four days later.

From then on, Giannis Antetokounmpo would score in double digits only five more times. The Milwaukee

Bucks were already well out of playoff contention with such a dismal performance the entire season. Giannis' best performance after the midway point of the season was when he had 14 points on 4 out of 6 shooting against the Detroit Pistons on March 31. He would end the season scoring ten points in his final game, which was against the Atlanta Hawks.

In his first season in the NBA, the 19-year-old Giannis Antetokounmpo averaged 6.8 points, 4.4 rebounds, and 1.9 steals. He shot 41.4% from the floor, and it was evident that he still needed to refine his offensive skills. Nevertheless, he was named to the All-Rookie Second Team. His Bucks would finish the season with a 15-67 win-loss record, which was the league's worst record that year.

Giannis Antetokounmpo's first season was mostly full of low points, especially with the way his team played and because his minutes were initially not as good as he would have liked. But what was most important to the Greek Freak was that he got out of poverty and provided for his family by making it to the NBA. It was a story of a boy who used to peddle items in the streets of Athens turning into one of the most intriguing young stars in the league.

Despite seeing the success of making it big in the NBA, Giannis Antetokounmpo never forgot to look back at his humble beginnings and sacrificed for his family the same way his parents did for him. One of the most popular stories of Antetokounmpo's rookie season was when the young teenager purchased a PlayStation 4 for himself. It was a normal indulgence for a young man of his age. He would spend hundreds and even thousands of hours playing video games by himself or with his brother Thanasis, who was playing in the NBA D-League that season.[i]

Thanasis would say later on that Giannis felt guilty about the $399 he spent on the game console while his family was still in Greece struggling and trying to make their way to the US. He did not like that he was indulging himself with a luxury he could not afford when he was in Athens while his parents were barely surviving with 400 euros a month several years back. The guilt got to him to the point that he sold the PlayStation 4 to Nick Van Exel, an assistant coach for the Bucks. Van Exel payed the retail price, believing that his rookie needed every dollar for his family.[i]

The entire season, Giannis Antetokounmpo tried to limit himself to a daily per diem of $190 until the day he finally got his family to the United States. It was not difficult for him to do so. After all, he lived in poverty just a few months before he was drafted. However, he did have a lot of help. Teammates know of his struggles as a boy and would even pass a few dollars to him from time to time. Those very same teammates were even generous enough to furnish the Antetokounmpo apartment with their old furniture.

There was even a time when, before one of the Bucks' games, Giannis Antetokounmpo grabbed a cab to go to a bank to send all of the money he had with him back to Greece. However, he then realized he did not have any left to grab another cab to get to the arena for the game. He also did not want to ask any of the team's staff to give him a ride to the game. Instead, he started running to the arena.

Wearing his windbreaker and running down the streets of Milwaukee on an unusually cold day, Giannis Antetokounmpo got a mile in before a couple saw him. The couple, who turned out to be fans of the Bucks, asked the 6'10" skinny young man if he was the rookie named Giannis Antetokounmpo, to which the young man replied in the affirmative. The couple then gave the rookie a ride to the arena. After that, the Bucks' general manager told Giannis to never hesitate to call any of the staff or employees if he needed a ride.[i]

Giannis Antetokounmpo's rookie season was one full of first experiences and revelations that he would not have experienced had he not been drafted into the NBA, but his humble beginnings were never forgotten. It was what made him work harder to get better and learn. Everything was a new discovery for him that season. From the taste of peanut butter all the way to learning how to drive, Giannis was never hesitant to try new things and add a new experience into his life without forgetting what he had left behind in Greece. It would take three months into the new season for him to indulge into a new PS4 again after his family had already moved to the US.[i]

And with the success he was seeing that season, a part of Giannis Antetokounmpo wanted to experience the American Dream through the eyes of an ordinary person. He once revealed to Thanasis how jealous he was that his brother could interact with people at the airports and hotels.[i] He loved the interaction and would have loved the experience of getting to know people

47

and places rather than the come-and-go nature of being an NBA player. But for what it was worth, Giannis was happy to be where he was, though he was still in a state of disbelief at times.

Giannis Antetokounmpo was also happy to be in Milwaukee, though it was not the most ideal place to fulfill one's American Dreams. The 15-67 season record in his rookie year did not dampen his spirits and love for the team. In his own words, he wanted to stay in Milwaukee for as long as he could because it was where he fulfilled his dreams. He was afraid that his ambitions would disappear if he was somewhere else other than in Milwaukee.[ii]

Even as a rookie, Giannis Antetokounmpo had already shown flashes of a star's mentality. His close friend Ross Geiger, who worked as a video coordinator with the team, was often amazed at what he saw both in the videotapes and in real life. He noticed how well Giannis read plays and even people, and attributes it to how the Greek Freak lived his life reading body language when he was still peddling on the streets of Athens.[ii] It was those difficult times and experiences that made Giannis into what he is. Anybody could have his physical gifts, but not everyone could go through what he did and make it out stronger emotionally and mentally.

After that 2013-14 season, wherein the Rookie of the Year award eventually fell into 11th pick Michael Carter-Williams' hands, nobody expected that Giannis Antetokounmpo would eventually blossom into a star ahead of everyone else in a draft class that lacked star power. Giannis still had work to be done, especially on the refinement of his offense and body. But if the 2013 NBA Draft could be redone, nobody would be called crazy to pick Antetokounmpo as early as they could.

Working Under Jason Kidd, First Playoff Season

After one year of being a professional basketball player, Giannis Antetokounmpo would have to face and experience the bitter truth and reality that the game is a business built on people coming and going. His close friends on the team would leave him in Milwaukee. Geiger, the video coordinator, joined the Phoenix Suns. Assistant general manager David Morway, the one who taught him how to drive, signed with the Utah Jazz. The saddest part was when Nate Wolters, his best friend on the roster, was cut from the team. In essence, Giannis realized that business is still business though he saw everyone on the team as an extension of his family.[ii]

Giannis Antetokounmpo would also realize that he had to be mentally prepared for any criticism and adjustments he had to make from the demands of his coaching staff. The hardest criticism he had to take was when he was told he was not working hard enough. It was painful for him to hear that his efforts were not sufficient because that was what he thought he was never short of. In his words, you could tell him he did something wrong or that he made a mistake on the court, but telling him that he was not working hard was not something that he could accept.[ii]

Then there were the adjustments he had to make when new head coach Jason Kidd took over the team. One of the first few things that Kidd told Giannis was that he was not allowed to shoot three-pointers. For Antetokounmpo, he felt it as an insult and limitation to his abilities because he wanted to continue shooting three-pointers. Then there came the benching in the early part of the season. Primarily a starter in his rookie year, Giannis was a bench player in the first few games of the season. In his season debut, he had ten points on 3 out of 6 shooting in 24 minutes for the Bucks, who lost to the Charlotte Hornets that night.

Irate that Kidd did not allow him to shoot three-pointers and that he was given duties as a bench player, Giannis Antetokounmpo at first was furious at the coach because he thought that he did not know what he was doing. Then he checked Jason Kidd's background. He saw Kidd's accolades, which included multiple All-Star appearances, All-NBA selections, a Rookie of the Year award, an Olympic Gold Medal, an NBA championship, and a ranking that put him second all-time in assists. Giannis realized that Kidd's accomplishments alone were enough to let him know that he knew what he was doing.[ii] That was how the coach earned the young Greek Freak's respect.

Giannis Antetokounmpo would eventually regain his starting status. But even before that, he had already shown significant improvements. He had a then-career high of 18 points on 6 out of 11 shooting in 30 minutes off the bench when the Bucks won against the Memphis Grizzlies on November 8. Giannis followed that up with 14 points and nine rebounds three days later in a win over the OKC Thunder. Then, in a loss to the Orlando Magic, he finished with a new career best of 19 points on 9 out of 15 shooting. Those performances were enough to let Kidd know that the Greek Freak was worthy of being a starter.

In his third game as a starter that season, Giannis Antetokounmpo turned in a fantastic all-around double-double performance in a win over the Brooklyn Nets. He had 18 points, 12 rebounds, four assists, and three steals. At that point of the season, the Bucks had already exceeded expectations. They had won seven of their first 12 games of the season and were well on their way to break their pace from the season before. The change in coaching style made a significant difference along with how the Bucks utilized the youth of the improved Giannis Antetokounmpo and 2014 second overall draft pick Jabari Parker.

On November 22 against the Washington Wizards, Giannis Antetokounmpo recorded a new career high in points after finishing with 20 markers on 6 out of 11 shooting from the field. It was in that loss when he broke the 20-point mark for the first time in his career. But defenses later on focused on Giannis, who struggled in three of his next six games.

For the second time that season and in his career, Giannis Antetokounmpo again scored 20 points. He made 8 of his 11 field goal attempts in 31 minutes of play against the Los Angeles Clippers on December 13. That was a performance that came after he scored 18 and 17 points against the Dallas Mavericks and the OKC Thunder respectively.

After consistent performances in December, Giannis Antetokounmpo would have back-to-back double-double games early in January 2015. He had 16 points and a career-best 12 rebounds in a win over the New York Knicks on January 4. Two days later, he replicated his performance by going for 16 points and 12 rebounds again in a loss to the Phoenix Suns.

While Giannis Antetokounmpo's abilities and confidence only grew for the better in January, it was early in February when he showed flashes of brilliance as a future All-Star. On February 2, he had another double-double performance by going for 12 points and 12 rebounds in a win over the Toronto Raptors. Following that performance, he had a new career high of 25 points in a win over the LA Lakers two days later. Giannis made 10 of his 14 field goal attempts in that game. Antetokounmpo would top that performance on February 6 in a loss to the Houston Rockets. He had 27 points on 11 out of 16 shooting from the floor as well as a new career high of 15 rebounds. A day later, he recorded 14 points, 11 rebounds, and five assists in a win over the Boston Celtics before wrapping up a week, wherein he was named Eastern Conference Player of the Week, with 12 points, nine rebounds, and eight assists for what could have been his first triple-double game. He averaged 18 points, 10.6 rebounds, 4.2 assists, 1.0

steals, and 1.6 blocks while shooting 60% from the field that week.

During All-Star Weekend, the increase of international talent in the NBA demanded a change of format in the Rising Stars Challenge. It was Team World against Team USA. Giannis Antetokounmpo would be a member of Team World representing Greece and his native country of Nigeria. In leading the way for the international players, Giannis finished with 12 points, ten rebounds, five assists, four steals, and two blocks.

Shortly after the All-Star break, Giannis Antetokounmpo's streak of 12 consecutive games scoring in double digits ended. In that loss to the Chicago Bulls on February 23, he had 11 points and five rebounds. From January 27 to February 23, he averaged 14.7 points, 8.2 rebounds, and 2.9 assists while shooting over 50% from the field and over 81% from the free throw line.

It was also around the halfway point of the season when Giannis Antetokounmpo's role with the team increased significantly. Leading scorer Brandon Knight was traded to the Phoenix Suns before the trade deadline. Though the team replaced their starting point guard with reigning Rookie of the Year Michael Carter-Williams from Philadelphia, he was more of a playmaker rather than a scorer. And months before that, the Bucks lost Jabari Parker to a season-ending injury. Because of these factors, Antetokounmpo's role as a scorer increased dramatically.

On March 9, 2015, Giannis Antetokounmpo would have a new career high in points in a loss to the New Orleans Pelicans. He recorded 29 points on 11 out of 16 shooting from the floor together with five rebounds, four assists, three steals, and three blocks for another all-around effort for the Greek Freak. It was also in that game when Giannis started another streak of double-digit scoring. This time, it extended to 14 consecutive games.

One of the better performances that Giannis Antetokounmpo had in that streak was when the Bucks lost to the Nets in triple overtime on March 20. Giannis played 53 minutes that game while finishing with 23 points and 14 rebounds for another double-double performance. That was also the sixth time in his career that he scored over 20 points. He would finish that 14-game scoring streak with 11 points in a win over the Boston Celtics on April 3. He averaged 16.2 points, seven rebounds, and 2.9 assists while shooting 54.5% from the field in those 14 games.

At the end of the season, Giannis Antetokounmpo averaged 12.7 points, 6.7 rebounds, and 2.6 assists while increasing his field goal percentage to 49% primarily due to better shot attempts from the floor and his decreased attempts from the three-point area. While Giannis' improvements were great for the Bucks, what was even better was that the team had improved its record to 41-41 after a dismal 15-67 the last season.

They would qualify as the sixth seed in the Eastern Conference playoff picture.

Aside from the improvements to Giannis Antetokounmpo's game, what brought the Milwaukee Bucks to the playoffs was how Jason Kidd preached defense to a team he purposely built to be long at all positions. With the 6'6" Carter-Williams at point guard, the 6'8" Khris Middleton at shooting guard, 6'11" Antetokounmpo at small forward, and a combination of Ersan Ilyasova, John Henson, and Zaza Pachulia at the two big men positions, the Bucks were one of the longest teams in the league. Kidd utilized this length to their advantage by playing a suffocating and frustrating style of defense that limited opponents to the lowest field goals made in the league. They were also the eighth-best team in limiting opponents' scoring.

But the gritty Bucks would face an equally gritty Chicago Bulls team in the first round of the playoffs. It was surely going to be a defensive battle between two teams that gave no quarter on that end of the floor. And for Giannis Antetokounmpo, the young 20-year-old would finally know what it felt like playing in the tougher and more physical NBA playoffs.

Giannis Antetokounmpo would make his playoff debut on April 18 in Game 1 against the Bulls. In that loss, he had 12 points, five rebounds, and four assists while struggling offensively from the field against the tough defense of Chicago. He was even worse in Game 2 after finishing with only six points on 2 out of 11 shooting. However, he had 11 rebounds and four assists in that loss.

The Milwaukee Bucks would find themselves in a deep 0-3 hole after losing Game 3 at home. As gritty as they were, the Bucks forced two overtime periods before finally succumbing. But it was also in that game when Giannis broke out in the playoffs. Antetokounmpo finished the game with 25 points, 12 rebounds, and two blocks in 51 minutes of play. He also made 10 of his 22 field goals.

Despite being in an insurmountable deficit, the Bucks kept fighting against the Bulls. They managed to live another day by winning Game 4 in Milwaukee. Giannis finished that game with ten points and eight rebounds. The Greek Freak would contribute well again in Game 5 when he had 11 points and four blocks. Thanks to such a performance, Milwaukee tightened the gap to 2-3 and were in prime position to force Game 7. However, the Bulls got serious in Game 6 and clobbered the Bucks by as much as 54 points. In only 15 minutes that night, Antetokounmpo finished with five points as he saw his first playoff appearance cut short with that loss.

The Largest Point Guard in the League

One of Giannis Antetokounmpo's biggest weaknesses was his skinny frame. Growing up in poverty, his family could not always afford to feed a tall boy such as Giannis was when he was in Greece. He always looked like a beanstalk on the court because of his length coupled with what seemed like skin and bones. He lacked the muscle to bang bodies and physically keep up with the grown and better-fed players of the NBA.

Measured at 6'9" and 196 pounds during pre-draft, Giannis Antetokounmpo was coming into his third season in the NBA at just 20 years old but had grown to about 6'11" already. On top of that, it seemed like Giannis had spent a lot of time in the weight room and eating a lot of protein afterwards considering that he bulked up nearly 30 pounds of muscle over the offseason. What was once a skinny kid was now a young man with muscles ripping out of his arms. All of that training in the weight room and proper nutrition turned the Greek Freak into a monster of a young man.

The Bucks also added more size to the roster by signing center Greg Monroe from the Detroit Pistons.

At 6'11", Monroe was not the tallest center on the court, but he had arms that were just as long as Antetokounmpo's. With Monroe's addition to the lineup and with Jabari Parker coming back, the Milwaukee Bucks became a fearsome team because of the size and length they fielded at all positions on the court.

Giannis Antetokounmpo, however, missed the season opener due to a suspension he incurred in Game 6 of their playoff battle against the Chicago Bulls. Nevertheless, he made significant noise when he debuted in the 2015-16 season on October 30 with 27 points, nine rebounds, and three steals. However, the Bucks ended up losing that game to the Washington Wizards.

Two nights later, Giannis would show that all of the work he put in throughout the postseason and that the muscle he had packed had helped him with his offense. He scored 20 points on 8 out of 12 shooting from the floor while also grabbing nine rebounds in the process in that loss to the Toronto Raptors. A day after that, he had 21 points and eight rebounds when the Bucks won against the Brooklyn Nets. After starting the season with three 20-point performances, Giannis Antetokounmpo showed refinement in his offensive game. The Bucks would then win three consecutive games with Giannis scoring in double digits in all of them.

On November 14, Giannis Antetokounmpo capped off a nine-game streak of double-digit scoring when he finished with a double-double against no less than the Cleveland Cavaliers in a win. Matching up against LeBron James, he finished with 16 points and 11 rebounds. In his first nine games of the season, Antetokounmpo averaged 17.8 points, 7.2 rebounds, and 2.1 assists.

Five days later against the Cleveland Cavaliers, Giannis took his matchup with LeBron seriously after he outplayed the man considered to be the best in the world. Antetokounmpo shot a crazy 12 out of 15 from the floor and made all eight of his free throws to finish with a new career high of 33 points. He would outplay The King, who had 27 points in the contest. However, the Cavs exacted revenge for their earlier loss by winning that one despite the career game from the Greek Freak.

Despite the vast improvements shown by their marquee player Giannis Antetokounmpo, the Milwaukee Bucks struggled to get out of the gates strong in that season compared to the previous year. They started out their first 20 games winning only seven. This led to Jason Kidd experimenting with his lineup and offensive sets. After his hot start, Giannis would somehow drop in performance because of the lineup and schematic changes from the coaching staff.

On December 12, the Milwaukee Bucks did the unthinkable and improbable. The Golden State

Warriors started the season 24-0. They were unbeatable and undefeated through the first 24 games of the season. They rampaged through contenders and powerhouse teams alike on their way to that historic start. With the Bucks next on the schedule, it would seem like the Warriors were on their way to a 25-0 record.

But the gritty Bucks, who were 9-14 at that juncture of the season, fought hard against their powerful opponents without giving an inch both literally and figuratively. Milwaukee used their length to their advantage as they covered shooters and recovered to the open man with relative ease. Giannis Antetokounmpo was integral in that performance considering that, with his length and mobility, he could keep up with the perimeter players during pick and roll situations and make it frustrating for shooters to see open daylight.

Because the Bucks used their length to their advantage against a jump shooting team such as the Warriors, they completed the upset and handed Golden State their first loss of the season. Giannis Antetokounmpo was the all-around force that Jason Kidd needed in that win. Starting at the point guard position to frustrate the ball-handlers with his length, he finished with 11 points, 12 rebounds, and eight assists for a near triple-double. Performances like that made Jason Kidd consider putting Giannis at the starting point guard position permanently.

Six days later against the same Warriors team, Jason Kidd differed from the tactic he used in the previous game and started Carter-Williams at the point guard spot. The result was also different as Golden State exacted revenge on the Bucks for stopping their historic start to the season. Giannis Antetokounmpo, who started at the small forward spot, had 20 points and six rebounds that game.

On December 23, Giannis Antetokounmpo turned in another solid and efficient performance when he made 11 of his 13 shots to down the Philadelphia 76ers. He finished with 22 points, five rebounds, six assists, and two steals in that game. Six days later, he would have an incredible double-double performance against the Thunder by finishing with 27 points and ten rebounds in that loss.

Giannis Antetokounmpo's breakout performance for 2016 came on January 12 in a win over the Chicago Bulls. The Greek Freak made 10 of his 14 field goal attempts to finish the game with 29 points on top of the ten rebounds and five assists he recorded. That game was the start of what would become four consecutive double-double performances for Giannis Antetokounmpo.

Antetokounmpo would follow that performance up with 19 points, 11 rebounds, and six assists in a loss to the Washington Wizards a day later. He then went for a solid performance of 28 points on 10 out of 18 shooting together with a career high of 16 rebounds in an overtime win over the Atlanta Hawks on January 15. He rounded up the streak with 14 points and 11 rebounds in a win over the Charlotte Hornets just a day later.

Giannis Antetokounmpo would have two more games of scoring at least 20 points in the month of January. He would have 25 points and nine rebounds in a win over the Orlando Magic on January 26 before ending the month with 28 points, six assists, three steals, and two blocks in a loss to the Miami Heat three days later. He averaged 16.3 points and 8.1 rebounds for January while also shooting above 50% in those 15 games.

February was a more consistent month for Giannis Antetokounmpo when he started the first nine games of the month scoring in double digits. He would also have four consecutive double-double games in February. He started off with 17 points and 13 rebounds in a win over the Washington Wizards on February 11 before following it up with 19 points and 12 rebounds in a loss to the Hornets the game after the All-Star Break.

On February 20 against the Atlanta Hawks, Giannis Antetokounmpo's identity as a player suddenly changed. The Bucks were 11 games below the .500 mark and Jason Kidd wanted to try something new. Michael Carter-Williams had been on and off the starting spot from game to game that season. Kidd went with Antetokounmpo as the primary playmaker. Giannis led the win with 19 points, 12 rebounds, and three assists that game. But two days later, he truly made his mark as a point guard.

On February 22 against the Los Angeles Lakers, Giannis Antetokounmpo finished the game with 27 points, 12 rebounds, ten assists, three steals, and four blocks. That was his first career triple-double and it certainly was not his last. From that moment on, Jason

Kidd decided to make Giannis Antetokounmpo his starting point guard. The team did not talk about it that much, there was no verbal understanding between Giannis and his coach. They did not want to make a big deal out of it and pressure Antetokounmpo, who was only 21 years old at that time.

At 6'4", Jason Kidd was already a big point guard. He was making passes that guys three inches shorter could not. He finished his career as the second all-time leader in assists just behind John Stockton. But Kidd wanted to be taller than he already was. He wanted to be like Magic Johnson, who he believes saw passes that he could only dream of making. But seeing Giannis Antetokounmpo, Kidd realized that he could make the young Greek Freak into the weapon he could not be when he was still playing. Jason Kidd embarked on a project to build the biggest point guard the league has ever seen.

At 6'11" and with arms that stretch as much as 7'4", Giannis Antetokounmpo was bigger than the 6'9" Magic Johnson and the 6'8" LeBron James, who would act as point guards in most plays. Jason Kidd started to put the ball in the large hands of the Greek Freak more often than he did before, and Giannis would not disappoint his coach in that regard.

After that triple-double outing against the Lakers, Giannis Antetokounmpo had a solid outing of 14 points, seven rebounds, and eight assists against the Boston Celtics three days later, though the Bucks would lose that one. Then, on the final day of a momentous February, Giannis Antetokounmpo finished with another triple-double. He had 18 points, 16 rebounds, and 11 assists to go along with four steals and two blocks in that win over the Houston Rockets. For February, Antetokounmpo averaged solid all-around numbers of 16.8 points, 9.6 rebounds, and 4.9 assists.

Giannis Antetokounmpo did not stop impressing people as a point guard. He would have another near triple-double game in a win over the Minnesota Timberwolves on March 4. He finished that game with 27 points, nine rebounds, 12 assists, three steals, and two blocks. After that, he went into Oklahoma City to match the Thunder's Russell Westbrook's triple-double with his own. He had 26 points, 12 rebounds, ten assists, three steals, and four blocks. Meanwhile, Westbrook finished with 15 points, ten rebounds, 11 assists, and a win for his team.

On March 13 in a win over the Brooklyn Nets, Giannis Antetokounmpo became the first Bucks player to have four triple-doubles in a season. He shot 12 out of 16 from the floor to finish with 28 points along with the 11 rebounds, 14 assists, four steals, and two blocks that he collected. With all the all-around stats he was putting up, Giannis was not only a triple-double monster but was also a defensive juggernaut for the Milwaukee Bucks. After that game, he would nearly have his fifth triple-double of the season when he finished with 18 points, 12 rebounds, and nine assists in a loss to the Toronto Raptors.

Giannis Antetokounmpo was an all-around beast at the point guard position for all of March. He posted fantastic numbers of 18.4 points, 7.1 rebounds, 7.2 assists, 1.5 steals, and 1.8 blocks while shooting over 50% from the field. At that moment, it looked like Jason Kidd's experiment was working and that Giannis was thriving more as a point guard for the Bucks.

Antetokounmpo would have his fifth and final triple-double of the season on April 1 after finishing the win over Orlando with 18 points, 11 rebounds, 11 assists, two steals, and three blocks. Two days later, he recorded a new career high of 34 points in a loss to the Chicago Bulls. He made 14 of his 22 shots in that game. Giannis continued to play well in the final five games of the season, averaging 18.6 points, 9.6 rebounds, and six assists as the campaign ended.

At the end of the season, Giannis Antetokounmpo averaged 16.9 points, 7.7 rebounds, 4.3 assists, 1.2 steals, and 1.4 blocks while shooting 50.6% from the floor in only his third season in the league. What was more telling were his post All-Star break numbers. In the 28 games following the midseason break, he averaged 18.8 points, 8.6 rebounds, 7.2 assists, 1.4 steals, and 1.9 blocks as the team's starting point guard. But despite his late-season push, Giannis could not hand a playoff spot to the Bucks, who finished with only 33 wins against 49 losses.

The Greek Freak Becomes an All-Star

After the stellar performances that Giannis Antetokounmpo pulled off as the team's primary point guard and ball-handler, Jason Kidd embarked on a quest to turn history's biggest point guard into an even more dangerous weapon. Not only would he announce that Antetokounmpo would become the Bucks' main ball-handler, but he also put the Greek Freak through training regimens and workouts that would make him an even more potent basketball player than he already was.

Kidd and everyone else on the team had been impressed by how Giannis Antetokounmpo knew how to play the point naturally. While everyone knows that it is easier for a player to put their head down and score as much as they want to, Antetokounmpo has been even better at making reads and finding open teammates for good scoring opportunities.[ii] With the way he plays, it was an obvious choice to make Giannis Antetokounmpo a playmaker and primary ball-handler.

Putting the ball into Giannis Antetokounmpo's hands also answered the Bucks' question on how he and Jabari Parker would play together on the court. Parker is a natural forward that could play the three or four positions. There would even be times when he and Parker might struggle with their identities considering that both of them can play either the forward spots. But with Giannis as the playmaker, it allowed Parker to play off the ball to find his spots.

The thing that made Giannis a natural playmaker was his understanding of his role as a ball-handler and slasher. Other point guards, most notably Kyrie Irving, Isaiah Thomas, and Damian Lillard, attack on the understanding that they would score the ball first. However, Giannis Antetokounmpo has a natural understanding that the purpose of driving to the basket is to make plays for others. This was why most of the Bucks' players only grew to become better scorers after the transition of Antetokounmpo from small forward to point guard.[viii]

Jason Kidd would have assistant coach Sean Sweeney to run a training program that involved having Giannis Antetokounmpo study a variety of film involving some of history's greatest players. The obvious choice would be clips of Magic Johnson. Sweeney had Giannis study

Magic's pick and roll while also deconstructing his own. And on offense, Sweeney had Giannis analyze the post moves of Kiki Vandeweghe while also having him watch clips of how Shawn Kemp plays the transition game.[ii]

Aside from letting Giannis study tape, Jason Kidd had him train twice a day for nearly three weeks. It was an unorthodox way of teaching him how to be a point guard. Sweeney would ask strangers to fill in for fast breaks and transition plays to help Giannis Antetokounmpo make decisions on the run. Kidd liked how that played out because Antetokounmpo showed point guard instincts by telling those strangers where they should be on the floor during the run. Had those been teammates of his, he would already know their instincts and habits. For Kidd, a point guard should tell his players where they should be for him to locate them.[ii]

The unique part about Giannis Antetokounmpo during that summer was that he turned down multiple offers from renowned trainers that have worked with some of the best players in league history. Instead, he put his trust in the Bucks' staff because he wanted to keep his circle of trust small. That was how he was brought up. His parents had to choose who to trust because they were illegal immigrants, and Giannis was the same. He decided to trust only those within his circle, keep a low profile, and keep his focus on what mattered most—getting better at basketball.[ii]

All of the hard work, growth, and improvements that Giannis Antetokounmpo had shown in three years with the Milwaukee Bucks showed how much raw potential the young man truly has. The scary part was that there was still a lot more left to unlock. Knowing how important Giannis was as the team's centerpiece, the Milwaukee Bucks would lock the Greek Freak in for four more seasons by extending his contract for $100 million.

Yes, this is the kid that used to peddle sunglasses on the streets of Athens and would sometimes come home empty-handed. This is the young man who had to get bribed with 400 euros a month just to play basketball. This is the very same teenager that got so guilty about the $399 he spent on a PS4 because his family was still in Greece living in poverty. But no longer did he need to sell cheap eyewear on the streets or live off 400 euros a month just to get by. No longer did his family's refrigerator have to be empty. And no longer did he need to feel guilty about indulging himself. All of this because he was now earning $100 million over the span of the next four years.

With all of the success and money he was about to earn, Giannis never forgot to be thankful for the opportunity and for whatever blessings that have come his way. He would personally call Bucks co-owner Wes Edens to thank the man for the money and for putting his trust in him as the team's future star player. He would then treat his friends and family to an expensive dinner as a means of celebration and thanks for the newly-inked $100 million contract.[ii]

But Giannis Antetokounmpo was not only growing in worth, skill, and physical capabilities. He was also quickly building up the confidence and cockiness needed of a franchise player. He was getting more mentally prepared for the game while getting pep talks from legendary players. Kobe Bryant once told him that summer was the most critical part of a player's season because that was when he could shoot thousands of jumpers eight hours a day every day. He told Giannis that early preparation in the summer was crucial for building on a successful regular season.[ix]

Even Kevin Garnett once joined the Bucks' practice to mentor Giannis Antetokounmpo, who shares a similar physical profile with him. These legends recognize greatness and potential because they know what it takes to get there. It would only be a matter of time before the world got to see how great Giannis was to become.

With Giannis Antetokounmpo's potential getting quickly unveiled before the world's eyes, the Milwaukee Bucks embarked on a new project that they hoped would follow in the footsteps of the Greek Freak. Holding the 10th pick of the 2016 NBA Draft, the Bucks decided to go longer by drafting the 7'1" power forward with a 7'3" wingspan, Thon Maker. Like Antetokounmpo, Maker was seen as a long-term project but one with the same potential given his equally impressive physical attributes. Along with Maker, the Bucks also added second-round draft pick Malcolm Brogdon, who turned out to be a steal, and free agent Matthew Dellavedova. Though Dellavedova started at point guard, the playmaking duties would fall on Antetokounmpo.

The moment the 2016-17 season began, Giannis Antetokounmpo's improved array of skills was in full force. Despite the opening day loss against the Charlotte Hornets, the Greek Freak seemed unguardable by any standards. He finished the game with 31 points, nine rebounds, and five assists while shooting 13 out of 21 from the floor in that opening match.

Antetokounmpo followed that performance up with 21 points, ten rebounds, three assists, two steals, and two blocks against a hapless Brooklyn Nets team in a win for the Bucks. And on November 1, he battled against Anthony Davis and the New Orleans Pelicans in a clash between two of the league's most mobile 6'11" players. Giannis finished that game with a win and 27 points, nine rebounds, and seven assists.

On November 12, Giannis Antetokounmpo would turn in a solid all-around performance in a win over the Memphis Grizzlies. He finished the game with 27 points, six rebounds, five assists, four steals, and four blocks. The next match, he had 26 points, 15 rebounds, and seven assists in a narrow loss to the Atlanta Hawks. And three days after that, he broke the 30-point mark for the second time that season by going for 30 points in a close loss to the league-leading Golden State Warriors.

On November 21, the game after that loss to the Warriors, Giannis Antetokounmpo would have his first triple-double of the season and his sixth career one when he finished a win over Orlando with 21 points, 11 rebounds, and ten assists to go along with five steals and three blocks. Then, four days later, he finished a loss to the Toronto Raptors looking like a legitimate point guard after going for 29 points and 11 assists.

Against no less than the Cleveland Cavaliers on November 29, Giannis Antetokounmpo thoroughly outplayed LeBron James in a win for Milwaukee. He finished the game with stellar numbers of 34 points, 12 rebounds, five assists, five steals, and two blocks.

Meanwhile, his superstar counterpart had 22 points, four rebounds, and four assists. Three seasons earlier, nobody expected Giannis to be matching up well with LeBron much less outplaying him. Now he does that to every other superstar in the league.

Giannis Antetokounmpo was named Eastern Conference Player of the Week on December 5 after the stellar numbers he put in the week leading up to that day. He averaged 24.3 points, ten rebounds, 6.3 assists, 3.7 steals, and 3.0 blocks in the three games he played from November 28 up to December 4. The Bucks won all three of those outings.

Shortly after getting that award, Giannis had his second triple-double of the season on December 7. In that win over the Portland Trailblazers, the Greek Freak had 15 points, 12 rebounds, and 11 assists while also finishing with two steals and four blocks. While it came at a loss, three days later, he had 28 points, 13 rebounds, and seven assists against the Washington Wizards.

He topped that performance against Washington by going for 30 points in back-to-back games for the first time that season. He first had 30 points, nine rebounds, five assists, and three steals in a loss to the Toronto Raptors. After that, he led the win against the Chicago Bulls with 30 points, 14 rebounds, and three steals. He would then score at least 22 points in the next 11 games to show his consistency as a scorer. Along with that, he also had five double-doubles in that stretch of games.

It was during that run when Giannis Antetokounmpo showed that he was the newest superstar in the NBA. On December 23, he showed the full variety of his offensive arsenal against the Washington Wizards. The Greek freak was showing it all. He was dunking off Eurosteps and putbacks. He was looking like Kareem with his hooks down in the paint while also looking like Gervin with his smooth finger rolls inside the lane. He made the pull-up midrange jumper look like a staple of his offense while also doing his best Dirk Nowitzki impression by doing a one-legged fadeaway. He did all of that while never forgetting to get his teammates involved.

As the dust settled, the Bucks won the game by 27 points. Giannis only needed a little over 32 minutes to make 12 of his 19 shots and 15 of his 17 free throws to finish with a new career high of 39 points. He also added eight rebounds and six assists all while the crowd was chanting, "Can't stop Giannis," whenever he was getting fouled or making difficult baskets look easy. After the game, teammate Tony Snell told him to stay out of the gym during Christmas as a way of telling him that he had already worked hard enough with the way he played in that game. But for Giannis, it was not yet enough.[ii]

As 2016 was about to end, Giannis left another great performance for fans to remember. In a blowout win over the Chicago Bulls on December 31, Giannis Antetokounmpo finished 35 points on 13 out of 19 shooting as well as nine rebounds, eight assists, two steals, and a career high of seven blocks. With the way he was playing all facets of the game, there was no denying how far the Greek Freak had come from being a skinny project back in 2013 to one of the most intriguing superstars in the world in 2016.

On January 4, 2017, his second game of the New Year, Giannis Antetokounmpo sent Knick fans packing when he hit a turnaround jumper to win the game for the Milwaukee Bucks in front of a hostile New York crowd. The Greek Freak finished with 27 points and 13 rebounds that game. Two days later when they hosted the Knicks in Milwaukee, he had 25 points to push his double-digit scoring streak to 14 consecutive games.

Giannis Antetokounmpo would have more fantastic outings after that. In a loss to the Atlanta Hawks on January 15, he had 33 points, seven rebounds, and six assists. Three days later, he poured in 32 points, 11 rebounds, six assists, and three blocks before getting named as a starter for the Eastern Conference All-Stars just a night after that performance. Giannis Antetokounmpo was second among frontcourt players in fan, media, and player voting for the East and trailed only LeBron James in that regard. One could say that Giannis was not only becoming the most famous frontcourt player in the East but could also be the second best frontcourt player in that regard already.

Giannis Antetokounmpo became Milwaukee's first All-Star since Michael Redd in 2004. And after more than 30 years, he was the first Bucks player to start in the All-Star Game. He also became one of only two Greek players to be named as an All-Star. The other one was Peja Stojaković, who was born Serbian but later acquired Greek citizenship.

Even after getting named as an All-Star, Giannis Antetokounmpo remained humble and modest about the achievement. He was always reluctant to talk about his All-Star start because it was not the most important task at hand. At that point of the season, the Bucks had a modest record. They were struggling to get to the playoffs and were trying to replace the productivity left behind by the injured Jabari Parker.

For Giannis, what was most important was getting wins. He said that one should focus on getting wins even though he may or may not make the All-Star team or get individual awards. Winning was what was most important for him because it felt a lot better for him. More importantly, winning not only made him feel better but it also made everyone on the team feel like they were a part of something great.[x] Antetokounmpo remained humble and selfless despite the achievement.

Just a few days before going to New Orleans to play in the All-Star Game, Giannis had a new career high in points on February 10. In that loss to the LA Lakers, he made 11 of his 20 field goal attempts and 18 of his 21 free throws to score a total of 41 points along with eight rebounds, six assists, two steals, and three blocks. And five days later, right before he left for the break, he had 33 points, nine rebounds, three assists, and four steals in a win over the Brooklyn Nets.

Nobody expected it, but Giannis Antetokounmpo was the Eastern Conference All-Stars' premier player during the midseason classic. The Greek Freak made 14 of his 17 field goal attempts to score 30 points, which were the most by any East All-Star that game. He only needed 23 minutes to score that many. However, his performance was overshadowed by the record-breaking 52 points that the West's Anthony Davis had that night.

After the All-Star break, Giannis Antetokounmpo immediately went back to work to try to salvage the season for the Bucks, who were fighting for the final spot in the East. On February 24, the Greek Freak had 33 points, 12 rebounds, three assists, and four steals in a loss to the Utah Jazz. Two days later, he followed it up with 28 points for a win over the Phoenix Suns.

The Greek Freak led a Milwaukee Bucks run early in March. Despite not scoring as much as he should have or even collecting triple-doubles, Giannis did as much as he could to help his team win six consecutive games from March 3 until March 11. His best performance in that stretch was when he had 32 points, 13 rebounds, seven assists, four steals, and two blocks in against the New York Knicks.

Later that month, he had two consecutive 30-point double-double performances in wins. He started with 32 points, 14 rebounds, five assists, and two steals in against the Sacramento Kings before beating the

Hawks with his 34 points, 13 rebounds, five assists, two steals, and three blocks on March 24, which was two days after. He ended the month with a near triple-double effort of 28 points, 14 rebounds, and nine assists in a win over the Detroit Pistons. The Milwaukee Bucks only lost four of their 18 games in March as they were trying to get a playoff spot.

Because of the successful team performance the Bucks had that month, Giannis was named Eastern Conference Player of the Month averaging 22.4 points, 8.4 rebounds, and 4.8 assists during March. He became one of only four Bucks players to be given that award. And before the season ended, he tied Kareem Abdul-Jabbar for most career triple-doubles as a Bucks player. He had his eighth career triple-double on April 10 by posting ten points, 11 rebounds, and ten assists in a win over the Charlotte Hornets.

When the season was done, Giannis Antetokounmpo was a monster among men for the Milwaukee Bucks.

He averaged 22.9 points, 8.8 rebounds, 5.4 assists, 1.6 steals, and 1.9 blocks for the season while shooting 52.1% from the floor. He would become one of only five players in NBA history to lead his team in all five major statistical categories and also finished in the top 20 in points, rebounds, assists, steals, and blocks.

With statistics like those, Giannis Antetokounmpo had surely proven himself as the newest superstar in the NBA. He was a do-it-all player that not only scored points in bunches but also made everyone on the team look better. The scary part was that he was still improving. The Greek Freak was only an improved three-point shot away from becoming the most unguardable player in the NBA.

Before improving even further on what was already one of the scariest skillsets in the league, Giannis Antetokounmpo had to focus on the task at hand. They first had to go through the Toronto Raptors in the playoffs. It was a battle between the third and sixth seeds, though the gap between those two teams was closer than anyone thought.

In Game 1 of their series against the Toronto Raptors, Giannis Antetokounmpo led his team to score an upset win and drew first blood by going for a new playoff career high in points. He finished the game with 28 points, eight rebounds, three assists, and two steals while shooting over 70% from the floor in that upset win for the Milwaukee Bucks. Though the Bucks would lose in Game 2, he had 24 points, 15 rebounds, and seven assists that night.

In Game 3, the Greek Freak had an efficient night for the Bucks, who thoroughly outplayed the entire Raptors team to the tune of a 27-point win. Giannis finished that game with 19 points on 7 out of 10 shooting from the floor. However, he shot a poor 6 out of 19 in Game 4 when the Toronto Raptors tied the series at two wins apiece.

Giannis Antetokounmpo singlehandedly tried to give the Bucks back the series lead when he scored a new playoff high in points in Game 5. He finished that game with 30 points on 12 out of 18 shooting. However, the Raptors took home the win and forced the Bucks to a do-or-die Game 6. Refusing to let his playoff appearance end in the first round, Giannis Antetokounmpo tried to force Game 7 by scoring another playoff career high. He had 34 points on 13 out of 23 shooting from the floor in Game 6. Despite that, the Raptors were the ones that came out triumphant and sent Giannis and his team packing.

Even after the tough loss to the Raptors in the playoffs, Giannis Antetokounmpo still expected himself to work harder than he had in his career. His goal was always to become of the best in the world though he could already be considered as such. For Antetokounmpo, playing basketball was useless if he did not have the goal of being the best. He was out there to play the sport and chase goals and not just to play basketball for fun. At just 22 years old, he still had so much room to improve, and nobody thought that he could improve so much the following season.

Reaching Elite Superstar Status

In his fifth year in the league, the 23-year-old Giannis Antetokounmpo was already showing how much he had grown and improved as an all-around threat. On October 18, 2017, his first game of the new season, he had an incredible effort in a win over the Toronto Raptors by going for 37 points, 13 rebounds, and three steals. And in the game after that, he had 34 points, eight rebounds, and eight assists.

Giannis Antetokounmpo was not done showing off early that season. On October 21, his third game of the regular season, he led a win over the Portland Trailblazers with a new career high of 44 points to go along with eight rebounds, four assists, two steals, and two blocks. He rounded up his terrific four-game start by going for 32 points, 14 rebounds, and six assists just two days later in a win over the Charlotte Hornets.

After starting the first four games of the season with a total of 147 points, Giannis Antetokounmpo broke Kareem Abdul-Jabbar's 1970-71 season franchise record of 146 points. And after Giannis finished his fifth game of the season with 28 points, ten rebounds, and seven assists, he had a five-game total of 175 points, 53 rebounds, and 28 assists. That ranked as the best five-game start in the history of the NBA.

Giannis Antetokounmpo had his second game of scoring 40 or more points that season on November 7 against the Cleveland Cavaliers in a loss. Despite losing the game, he outplayed LeBron James and finished with 40 points and nine rebounds. Then on December 4, he scored 40 in a loss to the Boston Celtics. He also added nine rebounds and four assists to his name that game.

On January 6, 2018, Giannis Antetokounmpo showed why he was becoming the most dominant player in the NBA since Shaquille O'Neal. He finished a win over the Washington Wizards with 34 points, 12 rebounds, and seven assists. Because of that achievement, he racked up 20 or more points and five or more rebounds for 27 consecutive games. That was the longest of such a streak since Shaq himself did it back during the 2000-01 season.

Giannis Antetokounmpo continued showing his dominance as the season went on. On January 15, he had his first 20-20 game by going for 27 points and 20 rebounds in a win over the Wizards. Then in a blowout win over the Brooklyn Nets on January 26, Giannis finished with 41 points, 13 rebounds, and seven assists. And right before the All-Star Weekend, he had a triple-double performance of 36 points, 11 rebounds, and 13 assists in a loss to the Denver Nuggets on February 15.

Because of performances such as those, Giannis Antetokounmpo made it to the All-Star Game for the second consecutive season as a starter. He was then chosen as a member of Team Stephen Curry. During the All-Star Game itself, he had 16 points in a losing effort to Team LeBron James.

After the All-Star break, Giannis continued his dominant performances. He had 14 double-doubles in his final 22 games of the regular season. And during that span, he never lost his scoring touch, either. Antetokounmpo only scored under 20 points six times in those final 22 games but made sure he was consistent as he never scored in single digits during that same span.

At the end of the 2017-18 regular season, Giannis piled up improved numbers for the fifth straight year. He averaged new highs of 26.9 points and ten rebounds while also registering 4.8 assists that season. On top of that, he piled up 42 double-double performances and showed improved shooting numbers of 52.9% from the floor and 30.7% from the three-point line. His player efficiency rating, the best measure of a player's performance during the regular season, was 27.3 and only fifth behind superstars such as James Harden, Anthony Davis, LeBron James, and Stephen Curry.

Because of how much he had improved in only a span of a year, Giannis Antetokounmpo jumped from being an All-Star to a legitimate superstar in the NBA. His numbers and dominance on the floor were on par or even better than some of the best players the NBA has to offer today. But for him to be truly great, he needed to lead his team against all odds during the playoffs.

The seventh-seeded Milwaukee Bucks faced the Boston Celtics during the first round of the playoffs. While many thought that it was going to be a quick victory in favor of the higher-seeded Celtics, especially after Boston took Games 1 and 2 even though Antetokounmpo averaged 32.5 points, 11 rebounds, and 7.5 assists in those games, the Bucks fought back hard.

In Game 3, Giannis only had 19 points, five rebounds, and six assists, but he played 27 minutes in a blowout victory in favor of Milwaukee. Then in Game 4, he finished another great win by registering 27 points, seven rebounds, and five assists. With that win, the Bucks tied the series at two wins apiece heading into Game 5 in Boston.

Giannis Antetokounmpo was his usual dominant self in Game 5. He finished that game with 16 points, ten rebounds, nine assists, two steals, and two blocks. However, the Boston Celtics won to take back the series lead. Giannis bounced back with 31 points and 14 rebounds in Game 6 to force Game 7. However, he was limited to just 22 points on 7 out of 17 shooting from the field as the Celtics defeated the Milwaukee Bucks in a tough seven-game series.

Although Giannis Antetokounmpo and his Milwaukee Bucks fought valiantly against the Celtics in their first-round series, it was still not enough for a superstar such as him. An elite player like Giannis should have done more. In that regard, the first suspect was his inability to hit jumpers on a consistent basis and on his insistence of shooting shots outside of his comfort zone.

Throughout the regular season, 54.7 of Giannis Antetokounmpo's attempts came outside of the painted area and 26% of his total attempts were beyond 16 feet. However, he only made about an average of 33.8 of the shots he took from outside of the painted area. In contrast to that, he was making 75.6% of the shots he took in the paint.

What those numbers meant was that Giannis Antetokounmpo was effective as a scorer only when he was near the basket. He struggled to make shots when they were outside of the painted area. The only thing that opposing defenses needed to do was take away his ability to get to the rim. And when they did so, Giannis was limited to using his jumper as his primary weapon of choice. That was a gamble that teams were willing to make when facing him.

So if Antetokounmpo wanted to take his game to the next level, he needed to either fix his jumper or make some adjustments to the way he was putting up points near the basket. And what transpired and changed in Giannis Antetokounmpo's game the following season was what got him to the pinnacle of individual greatness in the NBA.

The Dunking Machine, MVP Season

In an attempt to make sure that there was no way for opposing defenses to take away his ability to score the basketball, Giannis Antetokounmpo put in the necessary work during the offseason of 2018. One of the first things he worked on during the break was his body, which he had been working on nonstop ever since he entered the league in 2013.

During the free time he got in the 2018 offseason, Giannis worked hard on getting bigger and stronger, hoping to make himself a more unstoppable scorer in the paint. He spent much of his time in the weight room to add more muscle to his already impressive frame and physique. What that meant was that the unstoppable paint scorer called the Greek Freak was only going to be a more dominant player when he was near the basket.

From 222 pounds during the start of the 2017-18 season, Giannis Antetokounmpo bulked up over the offseason to an impressive weight of 242 pounds. That means that he added 20 pounds during the break.[xi] And what was even more impressive was that it looked like it was all lean weight and it did not seem like he packed on fat based on the photos he was posting during his workout routines.

For a paint scorer like Giannis Antetokounmpo, it was crucial for him to pack on a lot of added muscle mass and strength. Scoring near the basket was never a problem for Giannis Antetokounmpo. After all, using his length, athleticism, and ability to finish attempts against contact, he made 75.6% of his attempts from within three feet away from the basket.

However, the biggest problem in the Greek Freak's game was getting to the basket. He was always long, quick, skilled, and mobile enough to dribble the basket from the perimeter to the paint. But when defenses could keep up with his speed while also playing him physically, he had trouble getting to the basket to score in the paint. This was evident when the Boston Celtics' physical defense and capable wing players were bodying him up and keep up with him step by step to prevent him from scoring inside the painted area.

But adding a lot of muscle weight and strength could change all of that for Giannis Antetokounmpo. Using the added bulk could help him muscle his way through tough defenders that were just as quick as he is. It would also be very difficult for opposing defenses to push him out of the paint when he was fighting for position near the basket. And when he was working off the post, he could very well be an unstoppable force if he decided to power through his man.

When it came to rebounding, having a bigger and stronger Giannis could very well help the Milwaukee Bucks. During the 2017-18 season, Milwaukee ranked dead last in rebounding because they had no capable rebounders other than Giannis Antetokounmpo who used his superior length, athleticism, and mobility to secure double-digit rebounds for the first time in his career. But a stronger Greek Freak meant that it would be easier for him to get into position for rebounds. As such, it was also expected that he could grab more rebounds in the upcoming season.

Giannis Antetokounmpo's competitive side also manifested during the offseason. He received several invites to train alongside well-known NBA stars such as LeBron James and Carmelo Anthony, who both could help turn him into a more complete player. However, the Greek Freak declined the invitations because he did not feel like it was right for him to be friends with opposing NBA stars and then compete hard against them during the season.[xii] Some would say that such as mentality was "Kobe-like" because of how fierce of a competitor Giannis was becoming.

The Milwaukee Bucks also did their part to try to make things easier for Giannis Antetokounmpo. They brought in former San Antonio Spurs assistant coach Mike Budenholzer, who won Coach of the Year with the Atlanta Hawks back in 2015 when he led them to 60 wins, to become their new head coach after replacing Jason Kidd with interim head coach Joe Prunty in the middle of the 2017-18 season.

Back when he was coaching the Atlanta Hawks, Budenholzer was known for bringing in the unselfish pace-and-space style of basketball that the San Antonio Spurs are known for. Now that he was with the Bucks, it was going to be evident that he was going to try to fit the same style with the pieces that he had in Milwaukee. And unlike when he was coaching the Atlanta Hawks, the Bucks had a legitimate superstar player in the form of Giannis Antetokounmpo.

The Bucks maintained the same core of players while adding Brook Lopez from free agency to try to bolster their frontline and ability to space the floor because of the former All-Star center's newly-developed ability to hit the three-point shot with high accuracy for a seven-footer. What that meant was that the Bucks would have four players surrounding Giannis to space the floor so that it would be easier for him to score near the basket.

When the 2018-19 season began, it became evident that all of the hard work Giannis put himself through as well as the offseason changes that the Milwaukee Bucks made worked to make it easier for the Greek Freak to dominate the NBA and for his team to perform at a rate better than anyone had originally expected. Antetokounmpo was already playing at an elite level the last season, and during the 2018-19 season, he was playing out of his mind and looked like an all-time great.

On October 17, 2018, his first game of the season, Giannis Antetokounmpo put on a great all-around effort in a win over the Charlotte Hornets. He finished the game with 25 points, 18 rebounds, and eight assists. A week later, he had his first triple-double game of the season after going for 32 points, 18 rebounds, ten assists, two steals, and three blocks against the Philadelphia 76ers. Giannis started his first five games with five consecutive double-doubles and averaged 25.8 points, 15.6 rebounds, and 6.6 assists over that span. He was also responsible for leading his team to a solid 7-0 start.

The Greek Freak had another solid all-around effort on November 4 when he had his second triple-double of the season. In that 35-point blowout win over the Sacramento Kings, he only needed 30 minutes of action to register 26 points, 15 rebounds, and 11 assists. The highlight of that performance was when he showed the full package of his unstoppable offensive arsenal. He drove to the basket from beyond the three-point line and gathered it near the free throw line while seven-footer Kosta Koufos was bodying him up. But the Greek Freak exploded past his bigger and stronger defender and dunked the ball hard over Koufos using his long right arm and freakish combination of strength and athleticism.

Over the next seven games, Giannis had at least 20 points, nine rebounds, and four assists in all of those outings. Such efforts earned him the Eastern

Conference Player of the Month after he averaged 27.3 points, 12.9 rebounds, six assists, 1.5 steals, and 1.3 blocks during October and November. He became the first Bucks player to earn that award multiple times.

In a loss to the New York Knicks on December 1, Giannis Antetokounmpo registered a season-high in rebounds. He finished that game with 33 points, 19 rebounds, seven assists, three steals, and two blocks. Eight days later in a win over the Toronto Raptors, he tied that number by going for 19 rebounds together with 19 points and six assists.

On December 14 in a win over the Cleveland Cavaliers, the Greek Freak was at his freakish best. He finished that game with 44 points, 14 rebounds, and eight assists while shooting 14 out of 19 from the floor and 16 out of 21 from the free throw line. Simply put, the Cavs had no answer for him that night. But to be fair for Cleveland, no other team had an answer for Antetokounmpo that season as he used his improved strength and hunger for greatness to dominate his defenders and dunk over anyone who got in his way.

In his final game of 2018, Giannis Antetokounmpo had a triple-double performance against the Brooklyn Nets in a win on December 29. He finished that game with 31 points, ten rebounds, and ten assists. Then, a few days later on January 5, 2019, he had his first breakout performance of the New Year by going for 43 points and 18 rebounds in a loss to the Toronto Raptors.

On January 9, the Greek Freak had the second 20-20 game of his career while collecting a new season high in rebounds in a win over the Houston Rockets. He finished that game with 27 points, 21 rebounds, and five assists in a matchup that featured the league's top MVP candidates for that season.

Speaking of the MVP, Giannis Antetokounmpo was widely regarded as the leading MVP candidate for that season heading into the year 2019. It was not only because he was putting up great stats and dominating his opponents, but he was doing so at a much more efficient rate than he did the previous season. And what was even more crucial for his candidacy was that he was leading the Milwaukee Bucks to the NBA's best record at that time while also acting as the catalyst for his team on both ends of the floor. Everything seemed so effortless for Giannis that season.

An example of one of his effortless performances was on January 15 in a blowout win over the Miami Heat. What made that game so effortless for him was that he did not even need to do a lot for his team to win but he still managed to put up 12 points, ten rebounds, and ten assists in what was a triple-double performance for him. And what was even more impressive was that he only needed to play 25 minutes that game.

At the end of January, Giannis Antetokounmpo proved how fast of a rising star he is regarding his play and popularity. He was the top vote-getter in the Eastern Conference despite the fact that the East had other popular superstars such as Kyrie Irving, Kawhi Leonard, and Joel Embiid. Because he was the East's leading vote-getter, he earned the role of captain and was going to choose his own teammates for the All-Star Game.

But Giannis Antetokounmpo was not content with being the East's leading vote-getter. He still wanted to dominate the entire NBA to prove how great he was. Right before the All-Star Game, he had a series of dominant performances that showcased his phenomenal scoring ability. From February 2 to 6, he had three consecutive games of scoring 30 or more points. He capped that off with 43 points on 17 out of 21 shooting from the field in a win over the Washington Wizards. Then, in the final game before the All-Star break, he had 33 points, 19 rebounds, and 11 assists in a win over the Indiana Pacers.

The Greek Freak was the most dominant and outstanding individual performer during the All-Star

Game. Teammates were looking for him on almost all of their possessions because it was so easy for Giannis to finish off lob passes for great dunks. The highlight of the night was when he caught a bounce alley-oop pass from Stephen Curry and dunked it hard. It was a pass that only Antetokounmpo could finish as he caught the ball about two feet above the basket before flushing it through.

Giannis Antetokounmpo finished the All-Star Game with 38 points, 11 rebounds, and five assists to lead the game in points. However, he did not win the MVP award that night as Kevin Durant, who led a second-half comeback performance for Team LeBron, went home with that trophy. Nevertheless, his performance was enough for everyone to believe that Antetokounmpo was already near or at the top of the NBA concerning overall abilities as a superstar.

But the All-Star Game was not the cream of the crop when it came to Giannis Antetokounmpo's performances. On March 2, in a loss to the Utah Jazz, the Greek Freak finished with 43 points, 14 rebounds, eight assists, and two steals, and that was still not his best game during the final stretches of the regular season.

In a matchup against the Philadelphia 76ers on March 17, Giannis was in full freak mode. He was dunking over everyone in that game and was finishing strong against defenders that were just as big as or bigger than he was. He finished that matchup with 52 points, 16 rebounds, and seven assists. That performance gave him a new career high in points although it came in a losing effort.

But April 4, Giannis Antetokounmpo got his revenge against the Philadelphia 76ers. This time, he was doing it on both ends of the floor as this was arguably his best all-around performance that season. In that win, he had 45 points, 13 rebounds, six assists, and five big blocks. The biggest block he had was when he swatted away a shot by the bigger and stronger Joel Embiid. He blocked the attempt so hard that the gigantic Embiid fell hard on his back after getting rejected by the Greek Freak.

After an incredible and dominant regular season from Giannis Antetokounmpo, the Greek Freak once again improved his numbers almost across the board. He averaged career highs in points, rebounds, and assists by going for 27.7, 12.5, and 5.9 respectively in addition to the 1.3 steals and 1.5 blocks he had that season. He also shot the ball at a crazily efficient rate by averaging 57.8% from the floor the entire season.

If you look at Giannis' numbers that season, you would see how far he has grown as an efficient superstar. He was averaging ridiculous stats while playing only about 33 minutes a night after averaging 36 minutes per game in his previous three seasons. His per-36 minutes stats that season would have been 30.4 points, 13.7 rebounds, and 6.5 assists.

The Greek Freak's shooting numbers that season were also crazy. He was using his improved strength and the Milwaukee Bucks' improved floor spacing to get to the basket with ease and was shooting 57.3% of his shot attempts within three feet from the basket. That number improved from 45.4% last season. He was also making 76.7% of his inside shots and was proving that there was no ceiling to his ability to finish strong near the basket.

When it came to the advanced stats, Giannis Antetokounmpo was just as freakish. He led the NBA with a player efficiency rating of 30.9. He also led the NBA in win shares per 48 minutes after leading the Milwaukee Bucks to the NBA's best record of 60 wins and 22 losses. His numbers and the Bucks' performance all season long were the primary reasons why Giannis Antetokounmpo was one of the leading MVP candidates that season.

But numbers could not give justice to how dominant and improved Giannis Antetokounmpo was during the 2018-19 season. You had to watch his games and look at his body of work to appreciate his greatness and realize that the NBA has never had a player anywhere near Antetokounmpo's talent and style of play.

The way Antetokounmpo played during the 2018-19 season was similar yet somewhat so different from the style we have been accustomed to seeing him play. No, he did not develop a consistent jump shot from the midrange or the three-point. He strayed away from that part of the game and managed to focus on scoring in the inside. But as the previous seasons showed, he could not always get to the basket to score inside where he is most dangerous. So how did he manage to become such a dominant inside presence during the 2018-19 season?

There were plenty of factors. The first one can be attributed to the Milwaukee Bucks' improved spacing and ball movement. Under Budenholzer, the team almost always had four shooters surrounding the Greek Freak. That included their centers as the Bucks always had a big man capable of stretching the floor to make it easier for Giannis to dominate inside the paint. And if opposing defenses tried to throw double teams at him, he could pass the ball out to open shooters.

But as good as Budenholzer was in making it easier for Antetokounmpo to score inside, it was the work that Giannis put himself through during the offseason that ultimately made him into the dominant and unstoppable force that he became. He added a lot of lean mass and muscle strength without losing his explosiveness, mobility, and leaping ability. That made it easier for him to power through his defenders.

In the past, Giannis had no trouble scoring inside the paint, but the problem he faced was getting to the basket. But during the 2018-19 season, getting to the rim was a lot easier. Almost 58% of the shots he took that season were within three feet from the basket. He increased that mark because his improved strength allowed him to play better against physical defense. You often see him pushing through his defenders when he decides to get to the basket. And the most impressive part was that he was doing it against big power forwards and centers that all look helpless when Giannis is driving through them instead of just past or around them.

The best part about Giannis' improved strength was that it had become so easy for him to dunk the ball hard. From 161 made dunks from the previous season, that number jumped to 279 during the 2018-19 season. Moreover, in the last season, 12.2% of the attempts he took were dunks. But during the latest season, 24.6% of the shots he took were dunks. But you have to look deeper into those dunk numbers to truly appreciate how monstrous he had become.

The paint points that Giannis Antetokounmpo scored that season were the most that any player has had since Shaquille O'Neal back in the 2004-05 season. The Greek Freak has also had the most unassisted dunks by any player in the NBA since the 1996-97 season when, again, Shaq was dominating the league with his combination of sheer size and athleticism.

To put it numerically, Giannis was second in the NBA in dunks made that season, making 279 dunks in the 72 games he played or an average of about four dunks a game. Meanwhile, the leader of that stat during the 2018-19 regular season was Rudy Gobert, who had a total of 306 dunks in 81 games played or an average of about 3.8 dunks a game.

But what set the Greek Freak apart from all of the prolific dunkers in the NBA was his ability to get his dunk attempts without the direct assistance of his teammates. Out of the 279 dunks he made, only 58.4% were assisted. Meanwhile, 81% of Gobert's dunks were assisted. Out of the top ten dunkers in the league, only Antetokounmpo had less than 70% assisted dunks. And out of those top ten dunkers, eight players had 80% or more of their dunks assisted by their teammates.

What those numbers mean is that all of the top dunkers but Giannis Antetokounmpo needed to be set up by their teammates. They were players that mostly waited near the paint to finish drop passes or pick-and-roll players that had to roll to the basket and wait for a pass to get open dunk attempts. Meanwhile, Giannis could set up his own dunk attempts like Shaq did back when he was still in the NBA.

Like Shaq, Antetokounmpo was dunking hard in traffic without needing an assist pass from a teammate. Using his long limbs and explosiveness, he could easily dunk over several players whenever he was near the basket. At times, multiple defenders were already bodying him up or contesting his shot but Giannis could still power his way to punch the ball through the basket. Because of how dominant of a dunker he was that season, he earned Shaq's praise even though the legendary center rarely gives praise to other players.[xiii] He even earned the nickname "Superman" from the original NBA Superman himself.

Although Giannis Antetokounmpo's ability to make unassisted dunks was just as impressive as what Shaq could do back in the day, he did it in a much more different manner. O'Neal was a dominant center that mostly got his dunks by posting up his man and powering through them in the paint. Meanwhile, Giannis did it in all sorts of ways.

Antetokounmpo was also getting a lot of dunks by backing down his man from the low post, but the best way he was getting them was through getting to the basket. He is an unstoppable beast in transition, especially when he gets the rebound and dribbles the length of the floor to finish hard using his long limbs, terrific footwork, and moves such as spins and Euro-steps. He is so freakishly long and athletic that he can dunk the ball from one end to another using only four dribbles.

The Greek Freak could also get his dunks from half-court sets by driving past big but slow defenders or by powering through quick but smaller men. Giannis has even learned how to get close to the basket for dunk attempts by finding positions wherein he could simply get to the paint using one or two dribbles. Jason Terry, his former teammate and now a staff with the Milwaukee Bucks, said that he has never seen a player like Giannis because of how he could get a lot of dunks by starting from the inside instead of inside like Shaq.[xiii]

Giannis Antetokounmpo was so unguardable as an offensive player that season that he did not even have to improve his jump shot to become the league's most dominant player. Adding a jump shot would not make him unguardable but would make him the biggest threat in the NBA. But during that season, what Giannis did as a pure inside scorer was already enough for him to be called the most unstoppable player in the league. But how did he get to that point?

His physical gifts might have been what initially brought him to the NBA, but what truly got Giannis Antetokounmpo to the dance from a skinny and raw foreign player to a leading MVP contender was his hard work. As Jason Terry put it, he has never seen a star player with the same kind of approach to improving his game as Giannis Antetokounmpo.[xiii] His work ethic was unheard of because of how dedicated he was to putting in the necessary effort to become greater than any other player in the NBA.

It was his humble beginnings and determination to give his family the life they never had was one of the things that motivated Antetokounmpo. He does not spend a lot of energy or money on trivial things that will not matter to his game in the long run. He does not care about looking good or getting the best sneakers because all that matters to him is winning games by becoming better than he was yesterday.[xiii] And because of that, he has reached heights that not a lot of players have reached as early as age 24. Even Shaquille O'Neal admitted that Giannis was better than he was at that age.

Thanks to Giannis Antetokounmpo, the Milwaukee Bucks headed into the playoffs with the NBA's best record. In the first round, they quickly defeated the eighth-seeded Detroit Pistons. Since the Pistons did not have the firepower to keep up with the Bucks because of how they were missing top scorer Blake Griffin, Milwaukee defeated them in four games. Giannis' best performance during that series was in the Game 4 clincher, wherein he had 41 points, nine rebounds, and four blocks in 32 minutes of play.

The Milwaukee Bucks faced the Boston Celtics, who had defeated them in the playoffs in the past, in the second round. Using their physical defense to take Giannis Antetokounmpo away from his comfort zone, they beat the Bucks the last season in a hard-fought seven-game series. And in Game 1 of their 2019 second-round series, it appeared like they had the Bucks' number as they were sending double teams to Giannis in the paint while playing him physically.

But after that Game 1 loss where Giannis Antetokounmpo only 22 points on 7 out of 21 shooting, he performed better in Game 2 by going for 29 points and 10 rebounds in a blowout win. Then, in a Game 3 win, he put the pressure on the Celtics' physical defense by drawing fouls. He finished the game with 32 points, 13 rebounds, and eight assists while shooting 8 out of 13 from the field and 16 out of 22 from the foul line. Milwaukee won that game as well.

Game 4 in Boston was another dominant display from the Greek Freak. Proving that the Boston Celtics' no longer had his number, he was able to power through their physicality and their defensive sets and went for 39 points, 16 rebounds, and four assists while shooting 68.2% in another blowout win. Then in Game 5, the Bucks completed a four-game comeback. Antetokounmpo had 20 points, eight rebounds, and eight assists in that 25-point win to help the Bucks advance to the Eastern Conference Finals for the first time since 2001.

In Game 1 of their East Finals series against the Toronto Raptors, the Bucks looked like the superior team and were fighting them well enough even without Giannis Antetokounmpo dominating. He finished that game with 24 points, 14 rebounds, and six assists. Game 2 was a different story but still favor of the Bucks as they blew the Raptors out by 22 points. The Greek Freak had his best output of the series by going for 30 points, 17 rebounds, five assists, and two blocks.

But Game 3 was an indication of how well the Toronto Raptors adjusted to defending Giannis Antetokounmpo. Using the athletic, strong, and mobile big man Pascal Siakam as the primary defender on Giannis to try to slow him down enough for the rest of the defense to recover and help out, the Raptors limited him to 12 points on 5 out of 16 shooting from the field in that win. It was a team effort for them as other players such as former Defensive Player of the Year winners Kawhi Leonard and Marc Gasol were quick to help out on Giannis whenever he could force his way to the basket.

It was almost the same story in Game 4 when the Milwaukee Bucks lost to the Toronto Raptors in a blowout. And in Game 5, the Raptors finally gained the series lead with a win over the Bucks. Using the same strategy, they were able to keep Giannis Antetokounmpo from dominating inside the paint by sending help defenders out and quickly recovering to open shooters whenever he passed the ball out to them.

Game 6 was the final indication that Giannis Antetokounmpo, no matter how dominant of a paint scorer he is, was still in need of a jumper. He struggled from the field and was forced to shoot from the perimeter. He ended up with 21 points on a bad 39% shooting clip as the Toronto Raptors completed the series comeback to win four straight games after losing Games 1 and 2.

The series loss to the Toronto Raptors was proof that neither Giannis Antetokounmpo nor the Milwaukee Bucks were finished products. The Greek Freak might have been able to dominate the regular season but the playoffs were different. During the postseason, teams go into overdrive on the defensive end and play a lot more physically than they do during the regular season.

The Raptors did a good job slowing Giannis down. They kept him out of the paint and made sure that his inside opportunities were tough by sending multiple physical defenders over to him. Because of that, Giannis averaged only 22.7 points on 44.8% shooting from the field and was forced to shoot more jumpers that he was accustomed to.

That said, it always comes back to Giannis Antetokounmpo's inability to hit jumpers on a consistent basis. While coaches believe that he does not need to become a great outside threat to become an unguardable player, it would still help turn him into an unstoppable force because teams would be forced to defend him a lot differently. Instead of taking away his drives or teaming up on him inside the paint, they would have to send multiple defenders on him out on the perimeter if he could hit jumpers with a lot more consistency.

Nevertheless, everyone knows that Antetokounmpo does not need to be Stephen Curry to impact games from the perimeter. But the least he could do was scare defenders enough for them to think twice about leaving him open on the perimeter to focus on keeping him outside the paint. It does not seem like much, but a consistent jumper can change a lot of things in how a team decides to defend a certain player.

Even though his playoff run did not end well, the season was not yet done with Giannis Antetokounmpo. As mentioned, he was one of the leading MVP candidates all season long and was a top-three finalist alongside James Harden and Paul George. But with all of the dominant performances he put up that season, was Giannis the most deserving of the awards?

Well, Giannis certainly had a good case for the MVP award. He was the league's most dominant and unstoppable force on both ends of the floor all season long. He even finished as a finalist for the Defensive Player of the Year award as well. And most importantly, the Milwaukee Bucks finished at the top of the NBA after improving their record by 18 wins from the previous year and jumping from the seventh seed to the first seed.

Giannis Antetokounmpo was the cornerstone of the Bucks' offensive and defensive systems. Because of the Bucks' improved offensive game and spacing, they ranked first in points scored, second in three-pointers made, seventh in assists, and fourth in offensive rating. This was thanks to Giannis' inside efficiency and how he attracted a lot of defensive attention to allow open shooters to get their shots up.

On the defensive end, Antetokounmpo was also the catalyst. The Bucks fielded capable perimeter defenders such as Eric Bledsoe, Malcolm Brogdon, and Khris Middleton. They also enjoyed how good of a post defender and paint defender Brook Lope is. However, the one that kept it all together was Antetokounmpo because of his ability to defend all positions and because he can play help defense better than almost anyone else in the NBA.

Giannis makes sure that teams are careful enough not to throw a weak pass whenever he is within the vicinity because of how his long arms can easily get steals. Whenever Antetokounmpo is near the paint, he plays the weak side really well and gets a lot of blocks by helping out on his teammates. And after stopping opponents from scoring, the Greek Freak knows how to finish defensive plays by collecting rebounds in bunches. That is why he ended up on the All-Defensive First Team in addition to his All-NBA First Team selection that season.

That said, Giannis Antetokounmpo was the one player that could impact both ends of the floor for his team at a level almost higher than anyone else in the league while leading them to the NBA's best regular season record. Other MVP candidates could score well while others only play defense out on the perimeter. Meanwhile, the Greek Freak was not only a dominant scorer but also the best all-around defender in the NBA. As such, he had a good case for the MVP award and was arguably the favorite to win it. That became a reality in June 2019, when Giannis was awarded MVP of the 2018-2019 NBA season.

Chapter 3: International Career

Giannis Antetokounmpo's first crack at international competition was when he represented Greece in the 2013 FIBA Europe Under-20 Tournament. He averaged eight points, 7.6 rebounds, and 2.2 assists in that tournament. Among all of the players in the tournament, he ranked second concerning rebounds. Giannis Antetokounmpo would help the Greek Youth Team finish the tournament as the fifth placers.

In 2014, the Greek Freak would be part of the Greek Men's Basketball Team that went to Spain for the FIBA Basketball World Cup. In that tournament, Giannis Antetokounmpo would average 6.3 points and 4.3 rebounds in the six games that he played. The Greek National Team finished the tournament with the ninth place while also hopeful about the growth of the then 19-year-old Giannis Antetokounmpo.

Giannis Antetokounmpo's next international tournament was when he participated with an experienced Greek Team in the 2015 Eurobasket. He would help Greece finish undefeated in the group stages as the team was quickly becoming one of the favorites for one of the three medal finishes. However, Greece faced a powerful Spanish team in the quarterfinals. Spain ended up winning that game. Giannis averaged 9.8 points and 6.9 rebounds in that tournament.

During the 2016 FIBA Olympic Qualifying Tournament, Giannis Antetokounmpo appeared in three games for the Greek team. In the game against Iran, he had 16 points. His best output was against Mexico when he finished the game with 21 points. And in the game against Croatia, the Greek Freak finished with only nine points and nine rebounds. He averaged 15.3 points and 5.7 rebounds in that tournament.

Chapter 4: Personal Life

Giannis Antetokounmpo was born in Athens, Greece to Nigerian immigrants Charles and Veronica Antetokounmpo. Both of his parents were professional athletes back in Nigeria. Giannis is the third of five brothers. His older brothers are Francis and Thanasis. The fourth brother of the bunch is Kostas Antetokounmpo while the youngest is Alexis. Thanasis used to play in the NBA Development League and is now in Spain playing professionally. Meanwhile, Kostas played for the Dayton Flyers and was drafted last overall during the 2018 NBA Draft. He played for the Texas Legends in the G-League and appeared for the Dallas Mavericks in two games. Alexis is now playing basketball at Dominican High School in Milwaukee.

Born as a child of illegal immigrants, Giannis Antetokounmpo had no citizenship when he was still growing up in Greece. He was neither Nigerian nor

Greek. It would take until May 9, 2013, before he went to the NBA for him to officially gain Greek citizenship. His name was formerly spelled Giannis Adetokunbo was officially changed to Giannis Antetokounmpo.

Chapter 5: Player Profile and Impact on Basketball

Giannis Antetokounmpo was drafted by the Milwaukee Bucks at the tender age of 18 years old. At that time, he was listed as a small forward standing 6'9" and weighing a little less than 200 pounds. When he was drafted, he was described as a raw prospect because of his unrefined offensive skills. However, the Bucks knew that he had potential coming into the NBA and was going to be a long-term project.

A few months into his rookie season, Giannis Antetokounmpo was reported to have grown more than an inch and was already standing a little over 6'10" and with arms at least 7'3". At that time, Giannis was seen as a defensive asset that was still developing as an offensive player. However, he showed flashes of brilliance as a future star player for the Milwaukee Bucks.

In his second season in the league, Giannis Antetokounmpo was playing the small forward and guard spots for head coach Jason Kidd, who often experimented with his lineup. Giannis showed significant improvement in his game while managing to hold his own against the league's top small forwards. At that time, Antetokounmpo was still far from the superstar he was destined to be but was already showing flashes of what he could potentially become in the future.

It was in his third season when Giannis Antetokounmpo began to rise as an NBA superstar. He grew to a height as tall as 6'11" and packed on a lot of muscle. Compared to the skinny beanstalk he was when he started in the NBA, Giannis Antetokounmpo had grown to pack tons of lean muscle mass after working out in the weight room and fixing his diet.

After playing the small forward position in the first half of the season, Jason Kidd started him at the point guard position post All-Star break after seeing what he could do as a playmaker. It was then and there when Giannis Antetokounmpo began his meteoric rise to stardom. His length, size, and talent as a playmaker convinced Kidd that he had with his team what would soon become the biggest point guard in league history. At the end of that season, Giannis' numbers increased across the board as he normed 16.9 points, 7.7 rebounds, and 4.3 assists.

Upon entering his fourth season in the NBA, Giannis Antetokounmpo put the tons of hours of work he went through in the offseason to good use. He improved his playmaking skills and offensive repertoire to fully develop into an NBA All-Star at the tender age of 22. He could defend multiple positions with his length and mobility. At the offensive end, he was a matchup nightmare that no player in the league could guard. He became an All-Star starter for the Eastern Conference while ending the season averaging 22.9 points, 8.8

rebounds, 5.4 assists, 1.6 steals, and 1.9 blocks mainly as a point forward for the Milwaukee Bucks.

During the 2017-18 season, he fully developed into a go-to player and had shown significant improvement as an all-around talent that could score tons of points, rebound at a high level, make plays well enough for a forward, and play great defense. His offensive repertoire showed refinement as he could get to the basket using guard-like dribbling moves and a Euro-step that was unstoppable and looked borderline illegal because of his length and mobility.

The way Giannis played that season was simply amazing. He was arguably the most unstoppable force whenever he gets to the paint because no other player has his combination of size, length, strength, and explosiveness. And because of that, he averaged a double-double of 27 points and ten rebounds as he continued to improve his numbers and his skills across the board.

But it was during the 2018-19 season when he became the most dominant force in the NBA since Shaquille O'Neal. Adding some strength and muscle mass to his frame, Giannis Antetokounmpo sported a lean body that was 242 pounds of pure and efficient muscle. Using his added strength, he bullied his defenders on his way to the paint. And knowing that nobody could stop him near the basket, he began to use his length and explosive more often than he did in the past by always looking to dunk the ball hard whenever he could.

Because of that, the Greek Freak turned into a Greek God because of how dominant he is inside the paint. He had the most unassisted dunks since Shaq back in the middle of the '90s and was always attacking the basket with fury and anger. Nobody in the entire NBA was a match for him as he was on his way to averaging 27.7 points, 12.5 rebounds, and 5.9 assists while shooting almost 58% from the floor.

While Giannis Antetokounmpo's drastic improvement had to do a lot with his work ethic and hunger to become one of the best in the world, his physical talents and attributes were what mainly brought him to the dance to become one of the most elite players in the entire NBA. Some would even consider his body as the ideal frame for basketball. Sports scientist Marcus Elliot once broke down the reasons why Giannis Antetokounmpo's body made him into one of the most intriguing stars in the league.[xiv]

First off, the assessment starts with Giannis Antetokounmpo's wingspan. So much of the game of basketball relies on angles. The best defenders would want to decrease an offensive player's angles to drive to the basket or to look for open teammates. This is where wingspan becomes a factor. A player with a longer wingspan can reduce driving and passing angles easier than most players. On top of that, they can get to places faster without moving their body.

With a wingspan of at least 7'3", Giannis Antetokounmpo denies driving and passing angles away from his assignment. He also gets to contest and block shots without having so much as to move his body compared to other players with shorter arms. And with his length, Giannis Antetokounmpo collars rebounds easier than most other small forwards. At his position, he is in the top ten concerning rebounding rate specifically because of his length.[xi]

When it comes to Giannis Antetokounmpo's lateral movement, he can move side to side faster and quicker than other players of his size. Lateral movement is a function of a player's hips. Stable and flexible hips mean that a player can help a player create a lot of lateral force whenever he gets his hips low.[xi] Throughout his NBA career, Giannis Antetokounmpo has shown that he could laterally keep up with the quickest players in the league because of the flexibility he has in his hips. A player with a quick lateral movement can defend better without fouling because his body can react to quick changes from the offensive player.

Giannis Antetokounmpo was first listed at 6'9" when he was measured during the pre-draft. However, he has since grown more than two inches to become a 6'11" small forward. He might even already be 7 feet. At that height, he poses a lot of matchup problems on the offensive end because no other small forward or point guard in the league can match up with his combination of mobility and size. The only player that could probably do so is Kevin Durant, whose height and mobility comes close second to the Greek Freak as far as small forwards would go.

Giannis Antetokounmpo's lean muscles have also helped him improve as an NBA player. He started out thin as a twig that could easily be overpowered by shorter players. However, the Greek Freak added tons of lean muscle to his frame without packing on mass. From 196 pounds, he now weighs 242 pounds of lean muscle that visibly pop out on the court even when he is not flexing.

The amount of lean muscle he added has helped his body keep up with the added weight. While most players that bulk up managed to slow down because of the amount of fat they also added, Giannis never lost a step in his mobility and athleticism because so much of the weight he added was lean muscle.[xi] The muscle mass and strength he added only served to make him stronger and more capable of absorbing contact whenever he attacks the basket with force.

So much of an athlete's power comes from his core. However, players that are bigger and longer have the tendency to have unstable cores that prevent them from having a stable center of gravity when getting low. However, Giannis Antetokounmpo has shown that he has the core stability of more compact guards. His core strength has enabled him to get low well on defense and have enough stability when dribbling the ball low, much like how guards do. His core strength has also helped him maintain his athletic ability in more complex movements such as grabbing rebounds and going for highlight-reel lob plays.[xi]

Having a great core has also helped Giannis maintain his balance whenever he is performing difficult moves that require your footwork and your core to be in perfect sync. One such example is his Euro-step, which he can do in traffic and all the way from the three-point line. Using his long limbs and his freakish reach, he can easily sidestep his way to the basket without losing his balance.

Giannis Antetokounmpo's hands are 12 inches long. Kawhi Leonard, who is famous for having large mitts have hands an inch smaller than the Greek Freak's. Wilt Chamberlain was reported to have hands that were 11.5 inches long. Meanwhile, Michael Jordan sported hands which were about as big as Leonard's. Giannis' hands trump all of those players.

With hands as big as his, Giannis Antetokounmpo can palm the ball with ease. He can handle it well with one hand while maintaining excellent control when dribbling it. By extending only one arm to grab rebounds and to palm the ball with one hand, he can get more extension than most players do when they go up for the rebound with two hands. The Greek Freak's mitts also help him finish well inside the lane primarily because of how well he takes care of the ball when going up for a shot.

So much of a player's athletic ability relies on his ability to launch from the floor at an instant. However, most players when going up vertically would have to re-gather themselves before they launch up for a dunk or rebound. Even the most athletic players take the time to go vertical. And when they can launch up in the air, defenders and other rebounders are already able to recover to them on time.

However, what makes Giannis Antetokounmpo the ideal athlete's body is that it takes no time for him to gather himself up and launch in the air for athletic plays. He can suddenly go up in the air off of long strides without even so much as to bend his knees up to gather enough force for a vertical leap. This is what has helped the Greek Freak get dunks easily of long strides and even Euro-steps. He gets putback dunks quickly than most other players do because of his ability to just launch him up into the air at an instant. It has been no wonder why he is often described as a pogo stick.[xi]

With all those said, Giannis Antetokounmpo's combination of length, lateral movement, height, lean muscle mass, hand size, core strength, and launching ability have all contributed to turning his body into the ideal basketball weapon. From an athletic standpoint, he can do it all because of how his body seemingly has no limitations.

Giannis Antetokounmpo can shut down defenders because of his wingspan and lateral movement. He can get physical and move efficiently because of his lean muscle mass and can finish well and control the ball with relative ease because of the sheer size of his hands. On top of all that, he can launch himself into the air quickly because of the power he has in his core and his long legs. All of Antetokounmpo's basketball skills have developed well particularly because he was blessed by the basketball gods with the tools to succeed at all facets of the game. It was also a bonus that he has maniacal work ethic to go along with the physical tools he was given.

It is like he took out bits of LeBron James' mobility and physicality and combined it with Kevin Durant's height and length while also adding Kawhi Leonard's hands to form the ultimate basketball player's body. As far as his physical attributes are concerned, the sky has always been the limit for Giannis Antetokounmpo. Judging by what he has shown, he is yet to scratch the surface of the vast potential that his body has in store for the basketball world to see.

Since the late '90s, we have been spoiled with what the new breed of seven footers can do out on the floor. We have seen Kevin Garnett moving with the grace of a small forward and shooting midrange shots like a guard. Meanwhile, Dirk Nowitzki took things to another level by shooting jumpers like he was a foot shorter than he really is.

During the late part of the 2000s, Kevin Durant took what Garnett and Nowitzki had and was a seven footer that could move, dribble, and shoot like a guard. Because of that, he has become the best-rounded scorer the NBA has seen in a long while and is continuing to rack his ascent as one of the league's all-time greats. Durant was the one that started this whole "unicorn" movement of players that have the size and length of power forwards and centers but also have the skills and mobility of guards.

There have been more unicorns that came after Kevin Durant. Names such as Anthony Davis, Kristaps Porzingis, Joel Embiid, and Nikola Jokic come into mind when it comes to some of the best unicorns in the NBA today. However, Giannis Antetokounmpo is by far the most unique unicorn out of the crop. He may even be the most unique player in the history of the NBA.

On top of how Giannis possesses the height, length, and strength of a legitimate NBA center, he possesses the speed and perimeter footwork of an all-time great guard. This allows him to move with the ball with so much fluidity and grace but also with the power of a freight train. While some unicorns prefer playing outside by shooting jumpers or making plays for others, Antetokounmpo is an entirely different breed of unicorn.

The Greek Freak often looks like a center because of how he dunks the ball hard against any kind of tough defense he sees. But the surprising thing is that he does so from the perimeter and makes his way to the paint instead of creating looks far from the basket. Nobody in the history of the NBA has had so much paint points and unassisted dunks while starting out on the perimeter instead of inside the paint. In that sense, Giannis Antetokounmpo is in a class of his own and is a unicorn that nobody is even close to.

With his potential still far from being fully unfolded, Giannis Antetokounmpo's impact to the game of basketball stems mostly from how he worked his way up from poverty all the way to being a $100 million player and into the Milwaukee Bucks' franchise player. Anybody else in the world can have the physical attributes that Giannis has. However, nobody else could have endured what he has gone through and work through adversity with the goal of being the best in his mind.

Born in poverty and as a young boy with no citizenship, Giannis Antetokounmpo lived in fear of being deported back to Nigeria along with his family. Because of his parents living under the radar in Greece, it was hard to find jobs. Giannis and his brother had to peddle items on the streets of Athens to help the family get by on a day to day basis. Sometimes, he would even come home empty-handed.

Basketball was Antetokounmpo's saving grace. He was discovered by a basketball coach, who had to bribe him with a job for his parents for him to join Filathlitikos' practices. He worked his way up from there until he became good enough to be noticed by NBA scouts. And when he reached the NBA via the Milwaukee Bucks, who drafted him, he was all potential and no skill.

Using his life in poverty as the fuel for his efforts, Giannis Antetokounmpo absorbed and learned everything he could to be a better basketball player. He worked day and night in the gym to the point that he would even spend three hours after losses to get better. It was this maniacal work ethic that helped him unfold portions of his potential season by season. Year after year, he improved his numbers and skills. Every season, his stats increase across the board because of how much work he puts himself through in the offseason.

By the time he reached his sixth season in the NBA, Giannis Antetokounmpo has transformed into an entirely different type of player. His body allowed him to absorb contact and dunk the ball hard whenever he could. He rebounds the ball so well that he often looks like an all-time great center when he goes up for a board. He is the league's most unique playmaker at the forward position because of how well he locates his teammates whenever he gets ganged up. And on the defensive end, Giannis can affect the game in many ways. He contests and blocks shots as a primary and weak side defender and also puts pressure out on the perimeter using his length and mobility.

The amazing thing about all that is Giannis Antetokounmpo is still in his mid-20s and is far from reaching his prime as far as athleticism and skills are concerned. His game is still on the rise and his maturity as a leader and as a superstar is still growing. And when he does reach the height of his physical and mental abilities, there might be no way to stop him from lording over the NBA.

But through all the success and the attention he has gotten in his rise to stardom, Giannis Antetokounmpo remained humble. He rarely talks about his accolades while making team victories the focus of his efforts. The Greek Freak keeps his circle of trust small as he prefers living low profile much like his parents did back in Greece when he was a young boy. And since coming to the NBA, he has never been tempted by the brighter lights and the huge dollars of playing in big markets such as New York, Los Angeles, or Chicago.

In many ways, Giannis Antetokounmpo has become the embodiment of the Milwaukee Bucks. He started small but worked his way up to become the face of the franchise and the league's most interesting young superstar. His humility and penchant for working hard are what Milwaukee is all about—a small market that prides itself on hard work. This is what has made Giannis Antetokounmpo an endeared part of the community.

This rise from obscurity and poverty into an intriguing franchise player is what Giannis Antetokounmpo has contributed to the world of basketball. He does have the physical tools that helped him succeed, but all of that would have been put to waste had he not worked himself up from his humble beginnings into a legitimate NBA superstar. The Greek Freak has become a model player for those looking to work their way up from the bottom all the way to the top not just in basketball but any other endeavor as well. Everyone has an untapped potential just waiting to be pulled out, and Giannis has shown that a little hard work is enough to reach out to whatever potential is in us.

Chapter 6: Future

Still in the middle of his 20s and just concluding his finest MVP-caliber season yet, Giannis Antetokounmpo still has several more years left in his career as a basketball player. His legacy in the NBA is still left to be measured given how young he is and how early in his career he still is. However, he has shown that he is quickly rising to become the top face of the Milwaukee Bucks franchise.

Already with a bunch of triple-doubles, Antetokounmpo has already tied Kareem Abdul-Jabbar's record in Milwaukee in half the games that the legendary center played with the franchise. While he still nowhere near the accolades of the league leader in career points, Giannis has shown that he has what it takes to follow in the footsteps of the man regarded as the best player to ever play in Milwaukee. And the way that the Greek Freak has been playing and improving for the franchise, it is not silly to think that he would someday rise to become the best Bucks player in league history.

With Giannis Antetokounmpo still quickly improving, rising, and climbing the ladder of the NBA's most elite players, one cannot measure how far he can reach once it is all said and done. The way he piles up stats and dominates his matchup every single night, he has reached a level of play that only MVPs are at. And if the Bucks continue to improve as much as he does every season, a championship might even be in store for him in the future.

With all of those uncertainties out, what is certain for Giannis Antetokounmpo is that he will continue to be one of the most intriguing stars in the league with the way he keeps on working on his craft and improve on his tools night in and night out. An All-Star starter at the age of 22 and a leading vote-getter at 24, Giannis would certainly stay on top as one of the best players the Eastern Conference has to offer. And the way he plays and pushes himself to become better, some already regard him as the best player in the NBA.

With as bright of a future as what is waiting in store for Giannis Antetokounmpo, it was the past that molded him and turned him into the successful superstar that he is right now. He worked hard for his family and himself in the hopes of rising from the bitter and challenging past that he, his brothers, and his parents had to live through. What this teaches us is that the past is what holds the key to the future. And for Giannis Antetokounmpo, it is what will ultimately turn him into one of the greatest basketball stars the world has ever seen.

Final Word/About the Author

I was born and raised in Norwalk, Connecticut. Growing up, I could often be found spending many nights watching basketball, soccer, and football matches with my father in the family living room. I love sports and everything that sports can embody. I believe that sports are one of most genuine forms of competition, heart, and determination. I write my works to learn more about influential athletes in the hopes that from my writing, you the reader can walk away inspired to put in an equal if not greater amount of hard work and perseverance to pursue your goals. If you enjoyed *Giannis Antetokounmpo: The Inspiring Story of One of Basketball's Rising Superstars*, please leave a review! Also, you can read more of my works on *Roger Federer, Novak Djokovic, Andrew Luck, Rob Gronkowski, Brett Favre, Calvin Johnson, Drew Brees, J.J. Watt, Colin Kaepernick, Aaron Rodgers, Peyton Manning, Tom Brady, Russell Wilson, Michael Jordan, LeBron James, Kyrie Irving, Klay Thompson,*

Stephen Curry, Kevin Durant, Russell Westbrook, Anthony Davis, Chris Paul, Blake Griffin, Kobe Bryant, Joakim Noah, Scottie Pippen, Carmelo Anthony, Kevin Love, Grant Hill, Tracy McGrady, Vince Carter, Patrick Ewing, Karl Malone, Tony Parker, Allen Iverson, Hakeem Olajuwon, Reggie Miller, Michael Carter-Williams, John Wall, James Harden, Tim Duncan, Steve Nash, Draymond Green, Kawhi Leonard, Dwyane Wade, Ray Allen, Pau Gasol, Dirk Nowitzki, Jimmy Butler, Paul Pierce, Manu Ginobili, Pete Maravich, Larry Bird, Kyle Lowry, Jason Kidd, David Robinson, LaMarcus Aldridge, Derrick Rose, Paul George, Kevin Garnett, Chris Paul, Marc Gasol, Yao Ming, Al Horford, Amar'e Stoudemire, DeMar DeRozan, Isaiah Thomas, Kemba Walker and Chris Bosh in the Kindle Store. If you love basketball, check out my website at claytongeoffreys.com to join my exclusive list where I let you know about my latest books and give you lots of goodies.

Like what you read? Please leave a review!

I write because I love sharing the stories of influential athletes like Giannis Antetokounmpo with fantastic readers like you. My readers inspire me to write more so please do not hesitate to let me know what you thought by leaving a review! If you love books on life, basketball, or productivity, check out my website at claytongeoffreys.com to join my exclusive list where I let you know about my latest books. Aside from being the first to hear about my latest releases, you can also download a free copy of *33 Life Lessons: Success Principles, Career Advice & Habits of Successful People*. See you there!

Clayton

References

[i] Wojnarowski, Adrian. "From Street Vendor to Surging NBA Player, Greek Freak Living the American Dream". *Yahoo Sports*. 18 March 2014. Web.

[ii] Jenkins, Lee. "Giannis Antetokounmpo: The Most Intriguing Point Guard In NBA History". *Sports Illustrated*. 3 January 2017. Web.

[iii] Chondrogiannos, Thodoris. " The Unlikely Story of Spiros Velliniatis, the Coach Who Discovered Giannis Antetokounmpo". *Vice Sports*. 27 April 2017. Web.

[iv] "How Giannis Antetokounmpo Went From a Scrawny, Hungry Kid to NBA All-Star". *Oregon Live*. 19 February 2017. Web.

[v] "Giannis Antetokounmpo". *Draft Express*. Web.

[vi] Harper, Zach. "Bucks' Giannis Antetokounmpo Isn't Done Growing Physically". *CBS Sports*. 2 December 2013. Web.

[vii] "Giannis Antetokounmpo". *NBADraft.net*. Web.

[viii] Weitzman, Yaron. "Giannis Antetokounmpo Turned Into A Real-Life Monstar When The Bucks Moved Him To Point Guard". *SB Nation*. 14 March 2016. Web.

[ix] Hansford, Corey. "Giannis Antetokounmpo Shared What Kobe Bryant Told Him In Post-Game Meeting". *Lakers Nation*. 8 January 2016. Web.

[x] Spears, Marc. "Giannis Antetokounmpo's first NBA All-Star appearance is just the first step in a promising career". *The Undefeated*. 17 February 2017. Web.

[xi] Windisch, Ti. "The Whiteboard: Giannis Antetokounmpo added 20 pounds of muscle folks". *Fan Sided*. 27 September 2018. Web.

[xii] Freedman, Isaiah. "Giannis Antetokounmpo turned down workouts with LeBron and Melo". *Slam Online*. 8 December 2011. Web.

[xiii] Davis, Scott. "How Giannis Antetokounmpo's jaw-dropping work ethic made him unlike anyone the NBA has ever seen". *Business Insider*. 26 April 2019. Web.

[xiv] Arnovitz, Kevin. "The Extraordinary Measures of Giannis Antetokounmpo". *ESPN*. 9 March 2016. Web.

Made in the USA
Coppell, TX
11 November 2019